GREAT BRITISH BIRDING EXPERIENCES

GREAT BRITISH BIRDING EXPERIENCES

Dan Brown

CONTENTS

Dedication

To my family.

Acknowledgements

A book like this is not produced without the conglomeration and dissemination of huge amounts of previously published information, individual input, personal exploration, and lots of patience from those around me!

A huge thanks must go out to every unsung hero who has helped compile atlases, bird reports, county avifaunas and the like, as well as to the county recorders who kindly provided me with information on the best bits of their counties. I could list hundreds of inspirational books and authors but special mention must go out to the BTO's *Bird Atlas 2007–2011* and also to Mark Cocker and Richard Mabey's *Birds Britannica*, both of which are seminal volumes in our understanding and enjoyment of birds in the UK.

A number of individuals were particularly unselfish with their time and generous with their information and advice, including Paul French, Dan Pointon, Garry Taylor, and most of all my father, Nigel Brown, who is the best sounding board possible when it comes to nature and writing.

I would like to thank Simon Papps and Reed New Holland for finally relinquishing to my pestering and publishing this book (and also having great patience with me); and similarly to my amazing wife, Rachael, who unfalteringly supported me throughout. Lastly to my amazing parents, as without them my passion for nature would undoubtedly not be what it is today.

Bird Names

The bird names in this book generally follow those compiled by the British Ornithologists' Union (BOU) in the eighth edition of *The British List* (2015), which is the official list of bird species recorded in Britain. There are a few exceptions, for example the use of traditional names such as 'Tystie' for Black Guillemot and 'Bonxie' for Great Skua.

INTRODUCTION

Birds are amazing. They elicit a complete spectrum of emotion in us. Some of us are fanatical about them, while others get passive enjoyment; we express awe at the phenomenal migrations and survival abilities of some species, enjoyment at the stunning plumage of others, pleasure at their elaborate displays, and even despair when a much-desired bird has flown before we get the chance to see it. It is a pastime that can capture the imagination of anyone; young or old, black or white, professors or plumbers, it really doesn't discriminate in any way, and between those of us who enjoy watching birds it forms a common bond.

We are exceptionally lucky in Britain to have one of the oldest and greatest cultures of birdwatching of any country in the world. Britain also has an incredible rich and varied avifauna which, over the course of a year, changes day by day. In many ways the variety of birding experiences the UK has to offer is almost unsurpassed, and the opportunities to enjoy them unparalleled. The UK floats on the eastern edge of the Atlantic, influenced by the Gulf Stream, Arctic winds, European high-pressure zones, and huge Atlantic depressions. It acts as an important breeding ground for many species travelling north each summer from sub-Saharan Africa; as a critical stop-over for millions of waders and wildfowl migrating along the East Atlantic Flyway, and as a safe haven in winter for huge populations of Arctic-breeding species that take advantage of the rich feeding and warmer climate influenced by the Gulf Stream. If you stop to think for just a minute you can come up with many amazing examples of where birds go to or come from to get to us. Swallows that migrate from the UK to South Africa across the Sahara, 200,000 Knot gathered on the mudflats of East Anglia on their way from the Arctic to West Africa, the Lesser Whitethroat that heads south-east to India for winter, Ravens that have occupied every niche available in the UK from the winter tops of the Scottish Munros to inner-city life, shearwaters that circle the Atlantic, phalaropes that spin a merry dance on tiny lochans on Shetland in summer but navigate to the Pacific for winter. The list goes on, and on, and on. And what's even more amazing is that that vast majority of these birds are easily

accessible to us. To say we live in a diverse and brilliant nation for birds is an understatement. If only more people appreciated it!

To compliment the amazing diversity of birds and bird behaviours we have in Britain, we also have an incredible network of charities, organisations, groups, and individuals, that work (often voluntarily) to understand and conserve our birds, communicate the many fascinating findings to us, the public, and be on hand to show us birds when we visit reserves. The RSPB, BTO, Wildlife Trusts, local nature reserves, county birding groups, Facebook pages, Twitter accounts, and news services all disseminate vast amounts of information and data on our British birds. Now more than ever we are fortunate

Page 6: Black-throated Divers are protected by law at breeding sites so care must be taken not to disturb them.

Above: Britain is phenomenally important for migrating and wintering waders.

Following page: We are fortunate to have a huge network of nature reserves in Britain, many with superb facilities. This is Rainham Marshes, Greater London.

to have huge amounts of information at our fingertips, which makes enjoying birds easier. Our conservation organisations own and manage huge areas of land across the country and many of their reserves feature in this book as brilliant places to encounter birds (for instance, 36 RSPB reserves and 10 Bird Observatories are highlighted). The BTO organises, collects, collates and publishes data on the status of our British birds, and much of this is collected by volunteers who devote their own time to expanding our knowledge and helping to protect an ever-diminishing countryside. One of the best things about enjoying birds in Britain is the ability to be able to give something back. Whether you are collecting data for a national survey, sharing news of your sighting among others, or helping someone with an identification in a bird hide, you are giving back and this makes the whole enjoyment of birding even greater.

As well as all the conservation efforts and data collection that goes on, there are of course many thousands of us who simply enjoy birding as a pastime. Britain boasts a rich and long culture of birdwatching. For as long as humans have documented life we have had a fascination with birds and birding. Over the decades it has developed, optics and technology have enhanced our enjoyment of birds, and our increased knowledge and ability to travel means that many more species and encounters are possible now than they were 50 years ago.

There is no better place to celebrate a mutual love of birds than the Birdfair, which is held annually in August at Rutland Water. This is a true melee of everything bird-related and sees anyone connected with birds and birding taking up a stand, whether selling bird food, outdoor clothing, optics, bird books or holidays. It's a great chance to meet people, learn more about the work of the various conservation organisations, listen to fascinating and inspiring talks, and help raise money for a good cause (every year a different conservation initiative is supported).

We should not forget that the populations of birds we enjoy are dynamic. As humans we generally fear change, especially change for the worse. While some bird populations are stable, many are decreasing and a considerable number are increasing. Britain has been massively modified by humans to the extent that very little

Above: Despite being persecuted to extinction a century ago we are now fortunate to have a healthy and increasing population of White-tailed Eagles in Scotland. This is an example of how conservation can be a success for both the species and for local communities as the presence of the eagles is estimated to have generated approximately £2 million per year from tourism.

Following spread: Whilst the Kingfisher is a stunning bird to enjoy, this book includes a number of lesser-known species and experiences to broaden the horizons of birders.

primary habitat still exists. A once wooded landscape is now dominated by intensive farming, complex infrastructure systems, and expansive conurbations. This has altered the composition and abundance of many species. Some species have taken advantage of our urban developments, such as Swifts and House Martins, while others expanded their ranges and became more abundant as agricultural activities increased, including Skylarks, Corn Buntings and Grey Partridges. The last three species have also suffered massive declines in population and contractions in their range as a result of the intensification of the farming activities that initially encouraged their spread. Some species, such as Cetti's Warbler and Little Egret, have seized upon the opportunities provided by changes in our climate to advance their ranges, while others, including Dotterel and Ptarmigan, are suffering for similar reasons.

With an increasingly urbanised country, it becomes even more important to make the effort to venture out in search of wild spaces, or even wildlife that has taken advantage of urban environments. Not all the experiences featured in this book require hours of travel, boats journeys, or dawn starts; some can be found right on your doorstep and that is where an enjoyment of birds begins.

This book is designed to draw together and celebrate some of Britain's most exciting, evocative and enjoyable birding experiences. Some experiences are pivotal in creating a sense of place and time. We tend to associate Chiffchaffs and Swallows with the beginning of spring, while Skylark song evokes a sense of openness, big landscapes and blue skies. An experience shouldn't necessarily mean a spectacle, but most bird-related spectacles are certainly experiences. Some experiences will be far more subtle; a day-to-day event that passes us by, a smell or unique sound, learning something new or mastering a new ID feature. Some will be well known, others less so. Some will be on your doorstep, others may require an element of adventure to guide your path. I thoroughly hope that those just starting out in birding will be inspired to get out and see more, while those who have been birding for decades may be able to relive some of their earlier birding experiences. It should serve as inspiration and enthusiasm to head into the field and enjoy birds as much as possible, every day.

The 40 experiences included here are a personal selection and do not necessarily represent the most popular. As a result I have omitted some superb experiences (for instance watching Peregrines hunt, or searching for Crested Tits in Caledonian pine forest) in favour of drawing attention to those that are less well-known (for instance soaking in the sights, sounds and smells of a night in a storm-petrel or shearwater colony).

Others highlight truly stunning parts of Britain and even elements of our history, such as the European Storm-petrel colony in the Broch on Mousa, and the dramatic natural harbour at Portree, Skye, and its resident eagles. The experiences also cover most elements of birds with some focusing on a particular behaviour such as display or migration, while others involved the spectacle of large numbers. I have tried to include experiences that stimulate all our senses, and others that highlight the need for conservation, citizen science and the great lengths that individuals will go to in order to champion a species. Some focus on a single species, while others celebrate our own passion for birds. It is far from an exhaustive list and there will no doubt be experiences you feel should have been included and others that you feel are not worthy of inclusion. This is one of the joys of birding; we all have our own favourites.

Unsurprisingly we tend to weight our experiences with birds heavily towards the visual elements, however our memories and enjoyment of the experiences are built on so much more, and some of the best birding experiences involve sound (lots of it), and even smell. Imagine, for a moment, a seabird cliff. Row after row of Guillemots or Gannets stacked hundreds of feet high on a precipitous cliff exposed to a tumultuous Atlantic swell. The image itself evokes a feeling of life on the edge, organised chaos, the struggle to survive and breed; yet the experience as a whole would be nowhere near as rich without the pungent smell of seabird guano, the clamour of thousands of birds, and the pounding of the ocean at the base of the cliffs. We often forget this, yet the way our brains work means that the memories formed when we stimulate multiple senses are far richer, and remain far more vivid for longer than those based on a single sensory function. Conversely we can also enhance a particular sense by shutting down others, for instance when listening to bird song try shutting your eyes. How about sticking your fingers in your ears and shutting your eyes at a seabird colony!? It sounds ridiculous but it works.

The single most important thing is that experiences should be yours.

How to use this book

This book features 40 British birding experience accounts. Each account includes a description of what it is you are hoping to experience, some background information, and the significance of the experience. Every account also has a section on when and where to experience it, listing key sites within Britain. Each one of these sites can then be cross-referenced with the maps that follow this section, and with the gazetteer (following the accounts) which provides further detailed information on how to get to each location. Where relevant there is also a 'Get involved' section which highlights how you can get more involved with conservation, data collection, or simply organised ways of enjoying the experience. The accounts have been grouped into: All year, Spring, Summer, Autumn, and Winter. Finally, following the gazetteer, there is a list of key organisations and businesses referenced within the book.

Above: Finding Crested Tits in the Scottish Highlands is one of Britain's many birding highlights.

Opposite: The thrill of a hunting Peregrine Falcon is an obvious choice for the top 40, but most people will already be well aware of this. I have focused on some of the lesser known experiences, and a few more well known ones in hope that while witnessing a kaleidoscope of wader flocks you may well witness a Peregrine in full attacking mode.

Safety

The great thing about birding is it gets you out in the fresh air. Needless to say this has the potential to put observers in harm's way, or even cause harm, so I encourage birders to remain safe. Some of these experiences involve nocturnal walks, huge sea cliffs, bogs and marshes, and farmland. All pose their own risk and each needs to be considered when out and about, especially when distracted by birds. Always bear in mind where you are going and act and dress accordingly. The last thing we want is for birders to be unearthed in 5,000 years time having stumbled into Hickling Broad and been preserved in the marsh. Please respect your own heath and safety, that of others around you, and that of the wildlife you are there to enjoy.

The Law

Many bird species are protected by law under Schedule 1 of the Wildlife and Countryside Act, which means it is an offence to disturb them while they are breeding. Social media in particular has allowed the sharing of many sensitive locations, and an increase in the popularity of photography as a pastime has also put some species under increased pressure, especially during the breeding season. All birders and photographers should err on the side of caution and not approach breeding birds too closely. Individuals witnessing acts of disturbance should also endeavour to stop the activity. A full list of protected species is available on the JNCC website at: http://jncc.defra.gov.uk/PDF/waca1981_schedule1.pdf

Some of the accounts featured within this book involve protected species, and the sites that are included are well-known, easily accessible sites that can be visited without causing disturbance.

Equipment

With all forms of birding, binoculars always serve to increase the enjoyment of any experience. A telescope can massively aid certain experiences such as seawatching or looking for eagles. If you are just starting out a good field guide is essential reading. If you want to push birding to the next level then you may want to think about recording bird sounds. This can be very rewarding, although you will require good quality equipment to make the most of this experience.

Opposite: Seabird colonies, such as at this gannetry, can launch an assault on all the senses.

EXPERIENCE ACCOUNTS

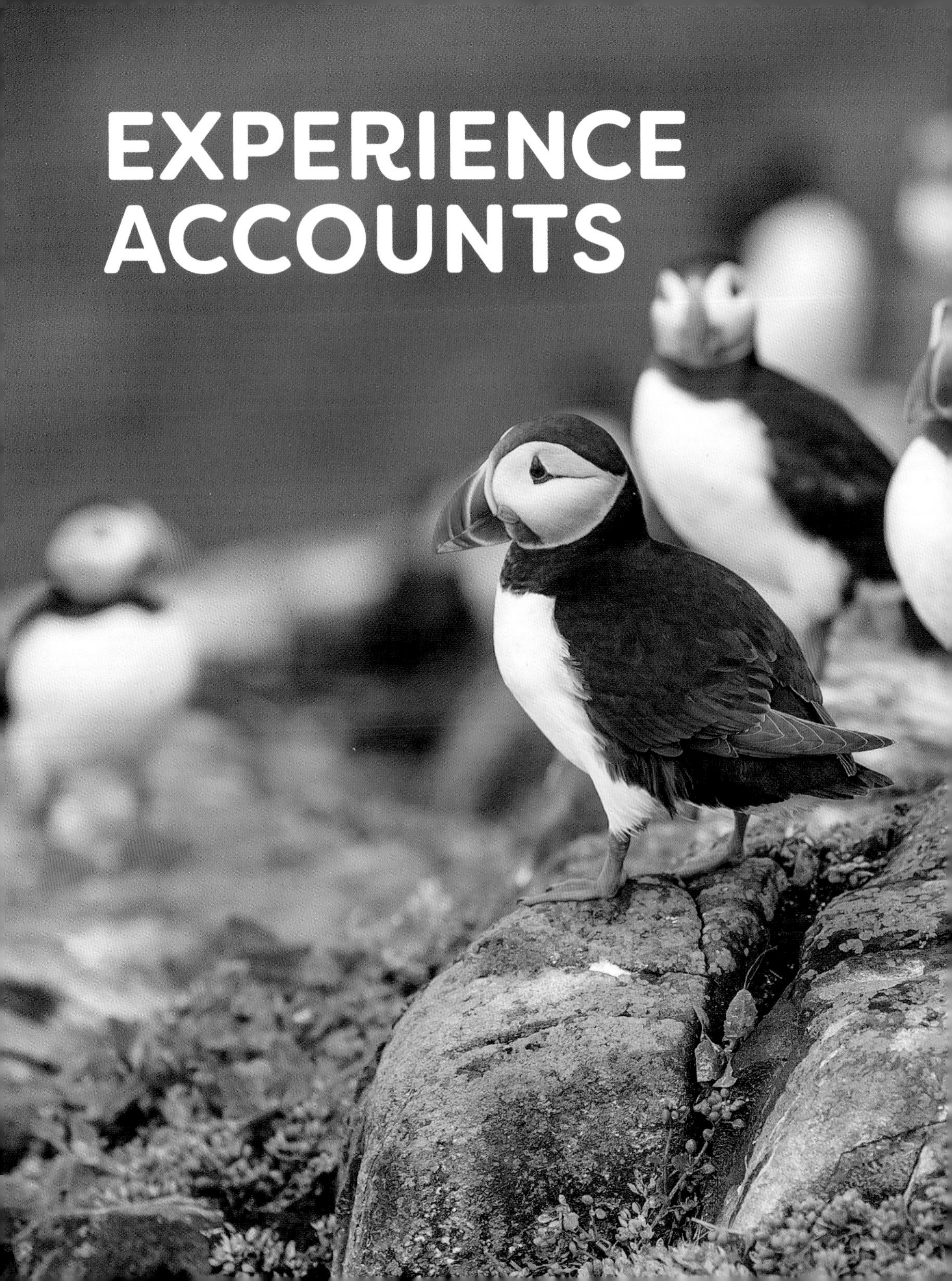

ALL YEAR

In late winter 2016 a Dusky Thrush was identified from photographs in the sleepy Derbyshire village of Beeley. It soon turned this hamlet into a hub of birding activity, whilst simultaneously raising funds for a local charity.

1. GARDEN BIRDS

You need look no further than your own garden for your first and one of the foremost birding experiences. In fact you may well be sitting reading this book with a view of your garden, or for those us without a garden, a window to the world outside. This is all it takes. Human interest in our natural world is innate – we are born with it. As children we want to know more, and as adults we continue to enjoy and learn. Currently I don't have a garden, but before I could speak I was transfixed by the birds I could see from the window at home. It started with colour and motion. Then a comprehension of different species, encouraged by my parents. This led on to keeping a list and recognising species that were different or unusual. A passion was born. Now as I type this my view from a top floor flat is very different to the garden I grew up in. My regular 'window' birds here in Glasgow include Goosander and Stock Dove, a flock of 600 Waxwings graced the tenement houses along the street a few years back, and the sight of Whooper Swans, a Peregrine, or Sand Martins still has my face pressed against the glass. Every garden is different and every one has its own avian story to tell.

One of the many pleasures of garden birds is being able to watch the intimacies of birdlife. From the moment-by-moment struggles of Blackcaps and Great Tits in securing a position at the bird feeder, to the first arrival of a brood of Great Spotted Woodpeckers, a fly-over Buzzard, a migrating wader heard from your bedroom window at night, or the bizarre world of Dunnock relationships. Outwardly Dunnocks are drab, brown garden birds that go largely unnoticed bar their eloquent song, yet they have a dark secret under their wing. These demure little birds are sexually deviant. The female forms the territory, attracting in one or more males who then defend it. She mates with up to three males and keeps them all on their toes, so much so that none can be sure of the paternity of the offspring and as a result all assist with the up-bringing. This bizarre behaviour even gave rise to a new word, polygynandry. It's amazing what goes on in quiet back gardens around Britain.

The element of surprise is enjoyable in any aspect of birding but the appearance of something unusual in the garden is particularly so. One of the joys of garden

birding is that even nationally common birds such as Fieldfare, Tawny Owl or Bullfinch can cause a moment of extreme excitement and pleasure when they turn up in your own garden. A classic garden 'rarity' is the Waxwing and this is such a great bird I feel it deserves an account all of its own (38).

As we continue to urbanise our country an increasing amount of land is being converted from vegetation to concrete and tarmac. Gardens are becoming increasingly important as wildlife refuges and form important corridors along which birds and other animals can move. It pays to think carefully about garden design – what we plant and where, and how we provide food and water for wildlife in order to maximise the positive impact out gardens

Above: Garden birds, such as this Robin, often allow close approach and the opportunity to study life histories. This in turn forms a connection in our brains between us, the observer, and the bird.

Following spread: Chaffinches and Greenfinches squabble over access to a bird feeder.

can have. Additionally we can now install a plethora of nest boxes, from those designed for colonial species such as Tree Sparrows to owl boxes and everything in between. It is even possible to get nest boxes wired up with internal cameras so you can enjoy watching the progress of a particular bird family on a second-by-second basis throughout the breeding season. As well as planting and designing for birds you also need to consider insects, as many breeding species will feed their young on invertebrates to begin with. The healthiest gardens will be the ones with mixes of native plants (which tend to attract the greatest numbers of insects), good feeding stations, multiple watering points and some mature vegetation in which to hide.

Garden birding is without a doubt the simplest and one of the most rewarding birding experiences we have. It can be experienced all year round and requires very little effort from us. Surprises abound and it provides the perfect window to observe the seasonal changes that occur. There is even the opportunity to get involved with simple citizen science projects including the Big Garden Birdwatch, organised by the British Trust for Ornithology (BTO), which occurs every February, as well as the Nest Record Scheme, also organised by the BTO.

WHEN AND WHERE

Year-round from the comfort of your home.

GET INVOLVED

You can get involved with the Big Garden Bird Watch at:
https://www.bto.org/volunteer-surveys/gbw
Check out the BTO, RSPB and Wildlife Trusts websites for tips on garden birds.
For advice on the best gardening practices and wildlife-friendly plants check out the Buglife factsheet:
https://www.buglife.org.uk/sites/default/files/Gardening%20for%20bugs%20-%20adults_1_0.pdf

2. MIGRATION

We automatically divide the year up into two migration periods, spring (March to May) and autumn (August or September to November), but in actual fact birds are on the move in every month. Migration is endless. Some are short migrations while others are epic journeys across oceans and continents. The UK is perfectly positioned to act as a hub to millions of migrant birds, in fact around 50 per cent of 'our' breeding birds migrate, from those travelling north and south between the Arctic, to those seeking to exploit Britain's productive summers before heading back to Africa. Many simply use Britain as a staging point and spend neither the summer or winter with us, such as Curlew Sandpiper and Little Stint – these are passage migrants.

There are other types of migrations too, and these include irruptions, with species such as Waxwing arriving en masse in Britain once food supplies have expired. Altitudinal migrations occur when birds

descend from higher breeding grounds to more affable lowland wintering areas. In many cases these migrations are not long but see a massive change in the habitat of the bird, for instance Snow Buntings breeding on the rocky plateaus of Cairngorm may spend the winter on the sandy beaches of East Anglia. Lastly we have partial migrants, those species which migrate in some areas but not in others. Here in Britain many species will remain resident all year as our climate is not too extreme. This includes the likes of Robins, Starlings and Chaffinches. Yet their continental counterparts will often undertake huge movements away from much more severe winter conditions, often swelling the numbers of commoner species in the UK.

Bird migration has long been seen as a harbinger of change. For birders certain species herald a shift in

Above: Lighthouses have always held a significance to migration watchers as they are often located on headlands which are key arrival and departure points for migrants. Many have now been converted into bird observatories, such as the one on the Isle of May, Fife.

Opposite: Geese are perhaps some of the most evocative harbingers of changes to the season.

seasons. Chiffchaffs, Wheatears and Sand Martins signal the arrival of spring and hopefully the exit of winter; screaming Swifts announce the start of summer; Green Sandpipers are the forerunners of the autumn migration; and the appearance of Goldcrests and the arrival of Redwings and Fieldfares mark the change from balmy early autumn days to stiff winds from the east. In fact for those of us with an interest in birds we can fairly accurately deduce the season, possibly even down to the week, by what we can see and hear around us.

Migrations do not just occur on a north-south axis, and in fact some of the most fascinating involve birds moving in very different directions. Woodcock for instance; a beautiful and cryptic wader, elusive in summer yet our most abundant wader in winter. These scalloped wonders spend the summer in central Russia, up to 2,800 miles (4,500km) east of where they spend the winter in the fields and forests of England, Wales and Scotland. Red-necked Phalaropes breeding on Fetlar, Shetland, have recently been found to migrate west to the Grand Banks off Canada at the end of summer before heading south down the eastern seaboard of the United States, then crossing over land in Central America to winter in the rich waters of the Pacific off the coast of Peru. A mind-boggling migration for such a tiny bird.

The realisation that much of the avian world around you is in continual motion puts a whole new perspective on birding and even adds an extra dimension to our day-to-day enjoyment of life. Imagine waking up and not recognising the song of the first Chiffchaff of the year?

Left: Tiny Red-necked Phalaropes undertake marathon migrations each spring and autumn.

Opposite: Arrivals of Fieldfares and Waxings signal the advance of autumn into winter as temperatures drop and days shorten.

WHERE AND WHEN

Typically from March to May and from August to November, although exact migration periods vary from species to species. Peak times for key groups of species include: April and September to October for warblers, May for skuas, July to September for seabirds, August to September for Swallows and martins, September to October for Goldcrest, October to November for finches and thrushes, and November for Woodpigeons.

Migrations occur across broad fronts often involving thousands if not millions of birds all moving simultaneously. Occasionally land topography funnels birds into concentrations before they have to make a sea-crossing. These sites offer the best chances to witness visible migration and include: Spurn, Yorkshire; Portland Bill and Hengistbury Head, Dorset; Great Orme in North Wales; and Duncansby Head, Caithness. In addition most bird observatories also offer opportunities. Many other sites, often seemingly non-descript inland locations, can prove important for migration, including many of the more prominent hills along the border of Wales and England. Visible migration has been monitored for a number of years at Hartshill Hayes, Warwickshire, and Gibraltar Point (Mill Hill), Lincolnshire.

GET INVOLVED

Why not visit a bird observatory, most of which have accommodation. You can find out more at: http://www.birdobscouncil.org.uk

In addition Spurn hosts the brilliant MigFest, an event celebrating bird migration. It comes complete with talks, ringing demonstrations and plenty of brilliant birding experiences. You can find out more at: http://spurnmigfest.com

Any bird sighting can also be recorded using apps such as Birdtrack and eBird.

Opposite: Migrating Lapwings often give hope to the end of winter.

3. TWITCHING

In the past twitching has rather unfairly been saddled with something of a bad reputation, and this is perhaps partly to do with a degree of confusion on the part of non-birdwatchers regarding exactly what twitching is. How frequently have you been asked what you're doing [birdwatching], only to be greeted with the response 'Oh, a twitcher?' For most non-birders there is no differentiation between the passive birdwatcher and the avid twitcher, yet within the hobby there is a world of difference. Thankfully in recent times most big twitches have been well organised, created good publicity for twitchers, and frequently generated income for good causes.

Twitching is the extreme competitive end of the birding spectrum. It is the desire to see a new species, to increase your list by one, not matter what, where or when. Twitching can occur on any scale from heading out to see a locally rare species on your local patch to dropping everything, chartering the first available plane and travelling across the country for a once in a lifetime event. No matter what the spatial scale twitching is very much an event of immediacy. Leave it too long and there is a greater chance of the bird vanishing; leave it a really long time and it becomes 'duding' rather than twitching – 'duding' is the act of casually going to see a rare bird, frequently long after it has arrived, rather than the immediate haste associated with a twitch.

Britain boasts an impressive bird list, between 600 and 620 species depending on the criteria used, but almost every year a new species or two are added to the list and a supporting cast of other exceptionally rare species turn up. These can be birds from just about every compass point, with extreme examples including Ascension Frigatebird from the South Atlantic, Black Lark from the steppes of Kazakhstan, Eastern Crowned Warbler from the Russian Far East, Allen's Gallinule from sub-Saharan African and Golden-winged Warbler from North America. These individuals are examples of lost birds and maybe pioneering individuals, often aided by exceptional weather conditions.

So what is it that drives those UK-wide twitchers? Well for many, if not all, there is the thrill of the chase. There is the possibility that the bird could just take

flight and continue on its journey, or simply swim around a headland and out of sight never to be seen again. Many a twitch has ended with the demise of the bird at the hands of the local cats, cars or Sparrowhawks. That race to get there before it moves on or succumbs is always fraught with anxiety.

There is a buzz to seeing a bird that is so ridiculously out of its range that you couldn't have imagined it ever turning up in the first place. Whilst this may spell doom for the single individual involved they can occasionally represent the fore-runners signalling a change in the migratory habits of the species – take Yellow-browed Warblers for example – and as pioneers they command even more respect from observers. In almost every

Above: Twitchers watching a White-tailed Lapwing at Rainham Marshes, Greater London, in July 2010.

case the individual bird has undertaken a monumental flight to get from where it started out to the UK – yet another astonishing achievement to be in awe of.

To be among the best twitchers there can be no hesitation. As soon as news breaks of a rare bird then all other activities must be curtailed and you must make every humanly possible effort to get to the bird. This can often involve journeys of multiple legs on boats, planes and helicopters, and it's not infrequent for a mega to turn up on Shetland, followed immediately by one on the Isles of Scilly, instigating a second twitch which spans the entire length of the country.

For many the experience also has an enjoyable social element – the feel of a community among the small band of folk who make the effort to see every new and exceptionally rare species in the UK. And of course there is the competitive element. Having the largest British list is something to be proud of and a remarkable achievement. So I encourage you to partake in even just one twitch to experience the rush, the thrill of the chase, to gaze in awe at the bird and what it has achieved to get there, and to savour the camaraderie between fellow twitchers.

WHEN AND WHERE

Rare birds can, and do, turn up anywhere at anytime so if you are wanting to start twitching then keep an eye on the news services (see below) and be ready to drop everything and go when news of a mega breaks.

GET INVOLVED

To twitch rare birds you need to keep up to date with the news. There is a plethora of media through which you can obtain information, including the long-established news services such as BirdGuides and Rare Bird Alert, however there are also plenty of good Facebook groups such as *Rare Birds of Britain and Ireland* and *UK Bird Identification*, as well as Twitter. If you have been lucky enough to find a rarity then please make sure you report it as fast as possible as the chances are there will be a lot of interested folk wanting to share your find.

Opposite above: Britain's first-ever Siberian Accentor, on Shetland in October 2016, was quite remarkably followed by several more records around the country in the next month.

Opposite below: It's four decades since the last twitchable Wallcreeper in Britain. If one was found today at an accessible site it would no doubt attract thousands of people.

4. FEATHERS

Feathers are the very essence of a bird, and therefore of this book even. They are vital for birds in terms of flight, camouflage, display and insulation. They can even create sound. We can tell which species we are looking and even how old the bird is by its feathers. You could say that a bird brings feathers to life, while conversely a lifeless dropped feather hints at the presence of a bird earlier in time.

Feathers are essentially glorified, modified scales. From the early ancestors of birds, the dinosaurs, scales have gradually adapted in shape, in colour, and in function. Most have become ultra-refined to aid flight and behaviour, yet some, especially in birds living outwith the UK – the kiwis and ostriches, for instance – have not evolved in such a manner.

If you are fortunate enough to own a microscope then it is well worth using it to examine a feather more closely. Two things become instantly apparent: first the intricacy of the feather's structure, barb after barb all interlocking to create a perfectly shaped unit; and second, pigmentation is lacking and the feather appears as shades of grey rather than a kaleidoscope of colour, which becomes apparent when light is shone on it from above. Even without a microscope, the combed leading edge to the primaries on an owl's wing are visible. These create lots of tiny vortices in the air and allow the owl to move almost silently, thus helping it maximise its hunting efficiency.

Being able to identify the different feather tracts greatly increases your chances of being able to identify the former owner of the feather. Feathers from different parts of the bird are structured slightly differently to maximise the individual's aerodynamism – these we refer to as tracts. The outer flight feathers, known as the primaries, tend to be stiffer, longer and more curved (both longitudinally and latitudinally). The shaft is also generally off-centre with a slimmer outer web and a deeper inner web. This creates a stronger feather which generates more lift. In comparison a secondary flight feather (from closer to the body) is a weaker feather being shorter, less markedly curved and with a slightly more flexible shaft.

An understanding of feather tracts is essential if you are interested in

understanding moult. Moult is the cycle of losing and replacing feathers on a bird. All birds must moult as feathers become old and worn and ultimately less efficient, costing the individual energy and potentially making it more susceptible to predation. There are several recognised sequences of moult which are described in great detail in other literature but as a very basic summary all chicks hatch with a coating of down. This is moulted into a juvenile plumage with which the chick fledges. Many birds, especially passerines (smaller perching birds), then moult out of their juvenile plumage into what is called a first-winter plumage – the plumage its acquires at the start of its first winter of life. It will subsequently moult into an adult-type plumage, although

Above: Close-up of Wryneck feathers. For an outwardly brown bird, the intricacy of the feathers is stunning.

with larger birds the sequence is much more complicated with different feather tracts being moulted at different times. This is particularly apparent in species such as Golden Eagle and White-tailed Eagle, where moulting all their feathers over a short space of time would prove fatal because regrowing feathers as large as an eagle's takes considerable time and energy. Instead they moult well-spaced feathers over a longer period of time, taking years in the case of eagles. This step-by-step moulting can be visible given good views and it can help with ageing birds accurately.

Even without an understanding of feather tracts and moult, finding and identifying feathers is great fun. From ad hoc discoveries to the regular checking of raptor plucking posts – the latter being a source of endless identification challenges – feathers are a fascinating sideline to birding and one which will certainly increase your skills and knowledge as a birder. The amateur study of feathers has even led to some fascinating insights in to nocturnal bird migration over the UK through monitoring the night-time predation habits of urban Peregrines by looking at prey remains each morning.

The study of feathers has been taken to new levels in recent years thanks to advances in DNA analysis. Feathers provide a non-intrusive and straightforward way of acquiring DNA which can help to determine the identity of an individual bird or how closely different populations are related to each other.

So next time you find a feather have a go at identifying its former owner and which part of the body it came from.

WHEN AND WHERE

Feathers can be found anywhere at any time. Some locations such as beaches and lake shores may hold larger numbers as tides and waves generally collect them. Plucking posts used by raptors are a great source of fresh and interesting feathers and they can also provide some revealing insights into the local diets of species such as Sparrowhawk and Peregrine.

Opposite: Pheasant feather detail. Even one of our most contentious residents must surely be admired for the beauty of its plumage.

5. PATCH BIRDING

The local patch is where birdwatching comes to life for most of us. It's often used as the first step into the wider birding world for those just starting out, while for those with years of experience behind them the local patch acts as a constant that can still throw up surprises, provide the regular delights of seasonal changes, and even enable us to develop affinities to individual birds or pairs that inhabit the site.

The local patch is as the name suggests an area of habitat close to home that allows easy and regular birding. It can be an estuary, woodland, gravel pit, headland or city park – literally anywhere, in fact. Patch birding is a great way for an observer to become familiar with the species present on their site. Many keep regular notes of numbers and species present, and even the activities of certain individual birds, and this no doubt leads to an increased enjoyment of the site.

The excitement of a new or unusual experience is heightened at places close to our hearts. As a teenager, before I

could drive, my patch was the Menai Strait – the short section of fast-flowing sea that separates Anglesey from the Welsh mainland. My section was the bit between the Britannia Bridge and the Menai Suspension Bridge. The place was brilliant, with a continual flux of migrants, occasional stray seabirds, and raptors flying over, while cold winters pushed Pochard and Shoveler onto the sea and Waxwings into the berry bushes. In 1997 a Little Egret appeared on the shore – a patch tick that marked an exciting advancement in the species' northward surge across the UK. In 2000 a pair raised three young on patch. The excitement of confirming this, of seeing the events unfold from start to finish, were some of the best and most rewarding of my birding life thus far. The patch hosted a pair of Sparrowhawks that frequently left clumps of plucked feathers around their favoured plucking stumps, and I would spend hours climbing trees

Above: The status of both Little and Great White Egrets has changed dramatically in the last 20 years. What changes will the next 20 years see?

Opposite: Shoveler – a widespread species but when one turns up in an incongruous location it suddenly becomes a mega!

Following page: Regular watching of a patch will yield prize after prize, in this case the chance to watch a brood of newly fledged Lesser Whitethroats.

Page 43: Finding a Red-flanked Bluetail is every patch-watcher's dream.

in search of nests. These experiences have entrenched themselves as some of my fondest birding memories, yet none of them involved especially rare species.

When we visit an area repeatedly we start to develop a unique and intimate understanding of the lives of the birds we are watching, from knowing which bush the Lesser Whitethroat will be signing in, to that birds' favoured feeding tree. Creating a connection in our brains with these birds intensifies our experiences and makes them more enjoyable. This experience becomes even more intense for us when we can observe the fortunes of breeding birds, from displaying adults to nest-building, eggs, the feeding of chicks, and hopefully fledging.

In some areas multiple birders will share the same patch. This can be superb in terms of generating some healthy competition, enjoying the more gregarious element of birding, and also sharing knowledge. It can even lead to some local-level twitching when a decent bird appears. In fact true rarities are not just restricted to well-watched local patches – finds such as a Red-flanked Bluetail in Gloucestershire, a Blyth's Pipit in Nottinghamshire, and an Eastern Crowned Warbler in Hertfordshire are all testament to that.

There of course scientific benefits to having a local patch. For one it makes selecting an area to conduct any one of the voluntary surveys run by the BTO, RSPB, or local ornithological society a much easier task, and secondly it should make the data gathered more robust given the observer's thorough knowledge of the site and the species present.

WHEN AND WHERE

One of the great things about patch birding is that it's a year-round event. You can watch your patch as often or as little as you like but you will undoubtedly begin to notice more small changes the more frequently you go and the element of wanting to return to see what else you can find often only increases with time.

Your patch can be anywhere and any size. From your back garden, town park or local reserve to a massive headland. Local patches are generally easily accessible to the observer. Check out an OS Map or Google Maps to find somewhere that you can call your patch.

GET INVOLVED

During the last few years the world of patch birding has taken on a competitive element through the Patchwork Challenge (http://patchworkchallenge.blogspot.co.uk). This light-hearted competition pitches local patchers against one another, and also against others with similar patches. With over 400 patches registered it's well worth getting involved and joining in the fun.

6. BIRD SOUND

Imagine a world without bird sound. If you close your eyes and listen you can often tell what time of day or year it is just by the sounds you hear. Owls calling at night, a strong dawn chorus, Swifts screaming, or the distinctive autumn *tut* calls of Blackbirds as they head to roost. We take bird sound for granted and nearly always focus on the visual element of birding but in actual fact the aural aspect is generally more important. Learn it and it opens a whole new door to enjoying birds. Up to 80 per cent of first detections during some bird surveys occur thanks to the identification of calls and songs, showing the importance of sound when recording birds.

Bird sounds have aesthetic appeal, conjuring a sense of place and often embodying the spirit of a location or habitat. Crystal-clear notes from Nightingales and Song Thrushes punctuate the air in the half-light, taking us straight to a woodland glade and inspiring composers and poets in the process. The less melodic *kyow* of the Herring Gull is probably one of the most instantly recognisable seaside sounds, and how about the *tseep* or *stüüüf* of a Redwing as it passes unseen overhead on a chilly autumn night. It's impossible to imagine walking into a woodland, reedbed or scrubland in spring without being accompanied by a cacophony of brilliant bird song, or a winter's evening without the murmurs of Starlings swirling in to roost. Bird sound inspires, evokes, enhances and alerts us.

Interestingly we often filter out calls we are unfamiliar with and either sub-consciously pass them by as something commoner or even fail to register them completely. Tracking down a species that is making an unusual call is a great way of learning bird sound. This, coupled with listening to bird calls on CD, digitally or online, really helps to expand your knowledge and the ability of your brain to detect new species. Websites such as Xeno-canto are perfect for learning a new species for instance, while the Sound Approach have published a number of books which focus on the importance of bird sound and come complete with CD recordings of these songs and calls. The first book in the series is by far the best and most comprehensive overview of bird sound and how to fully appreciate

and describe it. You can even learn how to read and describe sonograms.

Once you have developed a broader and deeper understanding of bird calls, the landscape and everything in it rapidly opens up. It's like learning a new language and then moving to a country where it's spoken. Alarm calls alert you to the presence of a Sparrowhawk that would otherwise have passed unnoticed behind you, while begging calls, social and feeding calls, and migration calls create a multidimensional environment.

While our visual acuity is weakened at night, our aural perceptions are sharpened. And darkness by no means precipitates the end of bird sounds for the day. Many birds call at night during migration and nocturnal migrants are not so fussy about their routes, frequently bounding over towns and cities. Standing outside your house on a calm, clear night in spring or autumn can often lead to some exciting additions to your garden list, from the more expected waders and wildfowl such as Greenshank, Whimbrel, Pink-footed Geese and Wigeon, to more exciting birds such as Quail, buntings and even flycatchers. You will undoubtedly also hear many calls that you can't identify; this is all part of the fun of listening to nocturnal migrants.

If you want to take it one step further why not try recording nocturnal bird sounds (and even diurnal bird sounds). It can be rewarding and eye-opening to identify all the species that pass over us at night.

WHEN AND WHERE

Everywhere and all the time. Bird sounds can be experienced wherever you live and at all times of day and night.

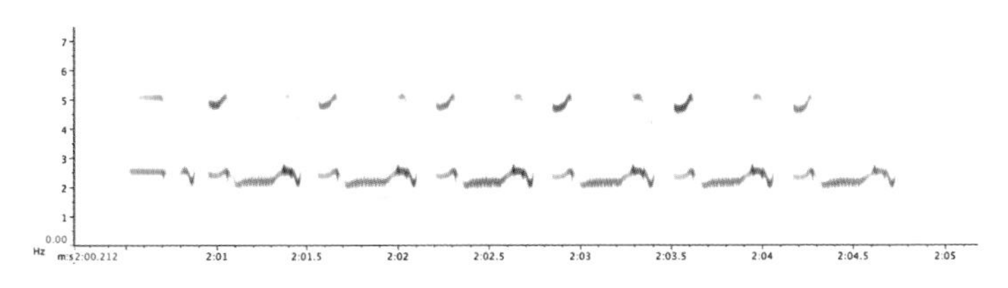

Above: A sonogram is a visual representation of a bird sound, in this case the warble of a Golden Plover.

Previous spread: Often regarded as the ultimate songster, an encounter with a Nightingale in full voice is undoubtedly one of the most divine birding experiences in the UK.

Opposite above: Sound is a vital part of our birding experiences, and familiarising yourself with the common species is a great way to start. Starling song is highly varied and full of mimickry.

Opposite below: Do you know how to distinguish Goldcrest and Firecrest (pictured) by their songs and calls?

SPRING

Pied Flycatcher is a classic British oak woodland species which is most easily seen in spring.

7. SPRING ARRIVALS

There's almost nothing as uplifting as the first returning summer migrants. The oh-so-sweet sound of a Chiffchaff singing from pussy willow and the first Sand Martins skimming low over gravel pits and lakes herald an end to the cold, dark winter and the start of warmer, longer days. These are the forerunners to the impending deluge of summer migrants that will flood across the country over the course of a few weeks in spring each and every year.

The first arrivals of Chiffchaffs and Sand Martins are often also associated with the first bumblebee and butterfly flights of the year – often including Brimstomes, Small Tortoiseshells, Peacocks, and maybe even Red Admirals – as well as with flowering Coltsfoot and Lesser Celandine and the budding of Hawthorn. It is a combined wave of change in the natural world that happens like clockwork.

As well as Chiffchaff and Sand Martin, Wheatear and Ring Ouzel are also among the harbingers of spring. The second pair forge a path up the western seaboard of Europe and can frequently be found back on snow-clad breeding grounds

in full song, often before the first Meadow Pipits have even returned to their upland haunts. For many people, non-birders especially, the appearance of Swallows is an important seasonal marker. This visual cue, an instantly identifiable icon of summer, has played an important role in amateur phenology records, with Swallows being generally more recognisable than more subtle species such as many of the warblers.

As more and more people move away from the countryside and into cities the connection with nature and species such as Swallows is being lost. People with an interest in birds and wildlife tend to take it for granted that we are continually reminded about the changes in seasons and weather patterns by the birds

Above: The Wheatear is one of the first spring migrants to return and they frequently arrive on territory when snow still lies on the ground.

Opposite: The Swallow is the most quintessential of British summer visitors and often the one by which people set their own seasonal clocks.

around us. I can't imagine what it must be like to walk out in spring and not register the sound of the first returning Willow Warbler or Blackcap, or to experience that joyous feeling that things are changing on a daily basis. Silent, grey and cold woodlands erupt into vibrant green jungles reverberating with sound in the space of a month. For returning birds the rush is on. Males sing to attract females and ward off other males, while females prepare themselves to breed. Nests are built, eggs are laid, chicks are fed, young fledge and in the blink of an eye spring has turned to summer.

For those just starting out in birding it can be an exciting but confusing period. A cacophony of sound confuses the brain and trying to pick out just one song can be almost impossible. Conversely as the day progresses and song activity quietens down it can be a good time to track down those unusual calls you hear.

For the more avid birder spring is nearly as exciting as autumn. The northerly flow of birds inevitably brings with it scarcities and even rarities from further south and east, and these frequently add a splash of colour. Bee-eaters and Hoopoes are becoming increasingly regular and occasionally breeding in this country, while the number of heron species occurring regularly has massively increased with Great White Egret now breeding annually and Purple Heron, Little Bittern and Night Heron all establishing toe-holds. If high pressure dominates over the Mediterranean then we can also see rarer species arrive and our common migrants are well worth scrutinizing more carefully.

WHEN AND WHERE

Typically the first spring migrants arrive in early March along the south coast and in general the earlier migrants work their way up the west coast first. A large flood of migrants appears in April with some of the biggest arrivals in the middle couple of weeks of the month. Our spring migrants can be found everywhere, but in order to enjoy the greatest variety and volume of song activity woodlands, scrub and marshes tend to be the most productive. Key migration points (see Migration chapter) will always see a greater number of actively migrating birds.

GET INVOLVED

Phenology – the study of seasonal natural markers – is playing an important role in understanding how the changing climate is affecting birds. Luckily it is exceptionally easy for us to note our first dates of spring migrants each year, so why not contribute to a national study and log your sightings on Nature's Calendar, a Woodland Trust project, at www.naturescalendar.org.uk

Left: The appearance of a drake Garganey always adds a touch of flare to spring birding.

Opposite: Coastal headlands such as Portland Bill, Dorset, are great places to watch migrants make landfall during spring.

8. DANCING GREBES AND DISPLAYING DIVERS

There is nothing quite like dancing Great Crested Grebes to enliven your day or even your week. The species was once hunted to the verge of extinction for the beautiful 'grebe fur' – the fiery orange and black mane that encircles the head like a ruff – but now free from persecution the population has bounced back to around 12,000 pairs. In spring they moult from their monochrome winter plumage into their more elaborate spring attire, fly back to their breeding lakes and start the show.

The performance begins slowly, after all it can last for up to four hours. The pair faces each other with grebe fur flared wide. They shake their heads and dip their necks backwards, preening with every dip. Each bird copies the other. One bird will dive down surfacing immediately in front of the other, necked stretched high, breast thrust out of the water and ruff fanned as wide as possible before slumping back down and engaging in some bill-tapping with its mate. The highlight of the display is the weed dance. The pair dives and gathers aquatic weed in their bills. Surfacing, they face each other with bodies held vertically, balancing on the surface of the water using just their massive paddle-like feet. Just centimetres apart, breasts often even touching, they slowly and deliberately shake their heads from side to side with the weed still in their beaks before finally slumping back onto the water. Occasionally the pair may even indulge in some water-running, with both birds paddling over the surface, bodies held clear, in perfect unison.

Divers can be equally impressive. Even when inactive, summer-plumaged divers are stunning to look at with spangled black-and-white plumage, shades of grey on the head and neck and a bold orange-red wedge of colour on the throat of the Red-throated. During the breeding season they can be particularly gregarious and in areas with a high density of breeding birds activity can sometimes become frenzied and even aggressive. Pairs will surge over lochs, much like grebes, paddling fast enough to thrust their bodies out of the water, head and neck outstretched. Head bobbing and shaking, neck thrusts and synchronous diving are all part of the choreographed display. Early in the season pairs and singles will indulge in large looping

display-flights over their territory, producing a *gwak* call as they go that can even sound like a distant goose at times. Black-throated Divers are even more vociferous, producing a far-carrying an eerie wailing and yodelling sound that seems perfectly suited to the huge, open and wild landscapes in which they breed.

Previous spread: Great Crested Grebe display is a beautifully elaborate and synchronous dance.

Opposite: Breeding-plumaged Red-throated Divers are simply stunning.

WHEN AND WHERE

Displaying Great Crested Grebes may be seen on any pond, lake or river supporting breeding pairs. They are widespread and common from central Scotland south to the south coast of England and any water body that has some aquatic vegetation is probably suitable for breeding. They can even be found on lakes in town parks, which makes enjoying this spectacle relatively easy. The best places to see this at close range include: Lochwinnoch RSPB, Clyde; Leighton Moss, Lancashire; Rutland Water, Rutland; and Hyde Park, Greater London. The displays are best seen earlier in the day although they can occur at any time, and peak months are February to April.

Our divers are listed as Schedule 1 breeding species and are therefore protected by law and making it an offence to disturb them while breeding. Most pairs are highly susceptible to disturbance although there are a few locations where breeding divers may be observed closely from public roads without disturbing them and these include: Loch Shin, Sutherland, and Lochindorb, Moray, for Black-throated Diver; and Mousa, Shetland, Dunnet Head, Caithness, and Loch Gowan, Sutherland, for Red-throated Diver. Another great place to find both Red- and Black-throated Divers, as well as summer-plumaged Great Northern Diver, is West Loch Tarbet, a sea loch on Kintyre, Argyll, where all three species can be found fishing in full breeding plumage. The best time to see these amazing displays is from April to early June.

9. DRUMMING SNIPE AND RODING WOODCOCK

Cryptic and elusive denizens of the half-light and darkness across marshes, woodlands and wet fields throughout the UK, Snipe and Woodcock are both common and widespread, yet our experiences with these birds are often fleeting. An explosion of russet and rufous as a Woodcock, the most adept woodland recluse, erupts from a tangle of bracken, branches or brambles and bats away through the trees; or the harsh rasp of Snipe as it bursts from wet ground, climbing with exaggerated and erratic zigzags until it is a mere speck in the sky. The sight of a flock of Snipe heading skyward gave rise to the collective noun; a wisp. Woodcock have long been known to arrive en masse on our shores with migrants descending on any bit of habitat as soon as they make landfall. These large arrivals were dubbed 'falls' and this term has persisted, being both the collective noun for Woodcock and also a general term used for any large arrival of migrant birds (see Migration chapter). In generally most of our encounters are in autumn and winter.

You might not realise it but Snipe and Woodcock are two of the most abundant wintering waders with an estimated 1 million of the former and 800,000 of the latter in the UK each winter. Many of these arrive on our shores from Scandinavia and north-east Europe, and even from as far afield as central Russia. Recent satellite-tracking studies have shown that these birds migrate on more of an east-west axis rather than flying from north to south. One bird was even found to be breeding east of the Ural range, close to the Kazakhstan border.

It is, however, in summer that both these species provide a very different experience as their typically skulking nature is enlivened by some brazen displays. With grunts, croaks and pops Woodcock patrol a route over the canopy of their territory in a slow-motion flight. They rarely give more away than an inky-black silhouette but this is enough to create quite a moment. Adjacent males will fly parallel and just occasionally a confluence of several territories will see an increase in the frequency of grunts, pops and *twisick* calls.

In contrast Snipe perform a high-adrenaline display. As if attached to an invisible roller-coaster a male Snipe arcs

and plummets, twists and turns, over open wetland landscapes, and in doing so produces a beautiful quavering sound, not from the vocal chords but through air causing the vibration of the stiff outer tail-feathers. This is known as drumming. It's a sound so often associated with the start or end of a day, calm weather, and wide-open areas of marshy ground.

Snipe have suffered population declines in their lowland breeding areas through the drainage of wetland areas and the intensification of agricultural activities. Similarly the Woodcock's UK breeding range appears to have retracted by at least 50 per cent in recent years and the species is now Red Listed as a Bird of Conservation Concern. It would be tragic to see these two iconic waders lost or reduced to pitifully low population levels in our time.

Above: Woodcock is perhaps the most stunningly cryptic of British bird species.

Following page: During April and May Snipe will occasionally 'sing' from fence posts, but their drumming display is far more exciting.

WHEN AND WHERE

In winter Snipe and Woodcock can be found throughout the UK. Snipe prefer areas of open wet ground including wet fields, watercourses, waterbody edges and marshes. Woodcock are most often seen in areas of cover, thickets and woodland during the winter, but at night they can be found feeding in damp fields or along forest tracks in wet woodland – anywhere that holds large numbers of invertebrates.

Both species are predominantly crepuscular, being most active in the half-light around dawn and dusk. Woodcock can be best observed in woodland clearings and forest rides which are on the routes of roding males, while Snipe are found in almost any area of open wet ground. Both species prefer calm weather and peak display activity occurs between April and mid-June.

Breeding Woodcock can still be found widely across the UK, although they are absent from many of the Scottish islands, south-west England and the Midlands, and are scarce in Wales. The best areas to experience the amazing roding courtship flights are: the New Forest, Hampshire; Breckland, on the Norfolk/Suffolk border; Blean Woods RSPB, Kent; the Peak District (Goyt Valley, Derbyshire); northern England, including Kielder and Hamsterley Forests; and areas such as eastern Scotland (for example, Mar Lodge), Speyside and the Black Isle. Smaller numbers can be found in Clocaenog Forest, on the Denbighshire/Conway border, as well the Brecon Beacons, south Wales.

Breeding Snipe are now most concentrated in damp upland areas including Dartmoor, Exmoor, upland Wales, and throughout the uplands of northern England and Scotland. Many lowland Snipe populations have now vanished but some persist in areas such as: Ouse Washes, Cambridgeshire; Somerset Levels (Westhay and Ham Wall), and Norfolk Broads. Moine Mhor, Argyll, can produce both species during the breeding season and in winter, not to mention a plethora of other wet woodland and marsh birds.

GETTING INVOLVED

Check out the Woodcock Network on Facebook, linked to www.ringwoodcock.net, for amazing Woodcock facts.

10. SKYDANCERS

I use the term 'skydancer' more loosely here than in its traditional context. For me there are four skydancers in the UK; Hen Harrier, Montagu's Harrier, Goshawk and Sparrowhawk. They are all species that perform exaggerated, highly-charged, almost frantic aerial displays above our hills, moorlands, farmlands and forests.

In their own right they are stunning birds when viewed well – perfectly designed for the habitat in which they hunt, with either short, blunt wings and a long tail for twisting and turning under boughs and between trunks, or longer, broader wings and buoyant flight for quartering over open ground. They are svelte birds, all possess long yellow legs capable of reaching out to grasp prey as it flees. The males of each species are a subtle blend of various tones of grey, slate, charcoal, lead, ashen and platinum, with each hue complimenting and accentuating subtle markings or focusing attention on their piercing yellow or orange eyes.

As with so many birds of the prey, the traditional skydancer, the Hen Harrier, has suffered massively at the hands of human persecution. Demonised by some who manage upland sporting estates as grouse-eating enemies of their livelihoods, they have become targeted to such an extent that on many upland moorlands which once supported breeding Hen Harriers, they are now nothing more than ghostly memories. The Hen Harrier is not alone as the other three species have also suffered persecution, especially Goshawks which, as they have recolonised and spread through the UK, have come into conflict with people who run Pheasant-rearing operations.

The displays of these species are something to behold. Perhaps those of the Hen Harrier, Montagu's Harrier, and Goshawk seem even more spectacular because of these species' rarity, but that of the Sparrowhawk is no less impressive. The male harriers circle upwards, generally into blue sky on beautiful spring days, before commencing their display over their preferred breeding locations. It starts with a burst of powerful downward-flaps which propel the harrier earthward. At its lowest point it jinks and, as if on a rollercoaster, is suddenly propelled skyward again calling with slightly agitated, slightly excited notes. As it reaches the top of its ascent it twists onto its back,

still flapping, and turns, falling, upside-down, back into its plunge, only correcting itself as it recommences its powerful downward-flaps before embarking on the next rollercoaster loop. This pattern of arcs and troughs can go on for hours in a bid to draw females into its territory, and is one of the quintessential sights and sounds of a British moorland.

The *Accipiter* hawks, Sparrowhawk and Goshawk, perform similar displays. The males rollercoaster over the woodlands that span their territory and frequently patrol the boundaries of their territories, often eliciting display responses from rival males. This can sometimes lead to multiple males all displaying over a small area. It's not unheard of in Wales to see nine Goshawks circling

Above: Montagu's Harrier is one of the most impressive skydancers; sleek, elegant and vociferous, but a very rare breeding bird in Britain.

Following page: The female Hen Harrier lacks the steely tones of the male so she can incubate less obtrusively amongst the heather.

and displaying in the same airspace. Both Goshawk and Sparrowhawk females also engage in aerial displays with some rollercoastering but they also eccentrically fan their white undertail-coverts and engage in a very slow and deliberate wing-flapping.

WHEN AND WHERE

Hen Harriers normally commence displaying in April, although occasionally some will start in late March, and they continue through until early to mid-May. Montagu's Harriers arrive later on their breeding territory and normally display in May and early June. Sparrowhawks can be found displaying from February through to late April. Given cold, clear days Goshawks will start displaying as early as January, although February to April are the key months, with March seeing the most activity.

Hen Harriers can still be found breeding in North Wales. At present they are very scarce in northern England due to persecution by humans. Better populations exist in Scotland, in the Southern Uplands, the Hebrides, Argyll, the eastern Highlands, Caithness and Orkney. Any area of healthy open moor is worth checking in spring but particularly good locations include Lake Vyrnwy RSPB, Powys, and Loch Gruinart RSPB, Islay, Argyll.

The Montagu's Harrier is an exceptionally rare breeding species in the UK with less than 10 pairs annually. Most nests are kept secret and all nesting locations are strictly protected, often outwith the public domain. However occasionally a nest will be suitable for viewing and publicised accordingly.

Sparrowhawks are widespread throughout the UK and can be found in and around any area of woodland, although they appear to be scarcer in places where Goshawks are present. Due to persecution by humans Goshawks became extinct in the UK by the late 1800s, but they have since returned and are slowly re-establishing themselves. Currently the highest densities can be found in Wales, with other populations in the New Forest, Breckland, the Peak District, the Scottish Borders and north-east Scotland. Key sites at which to witness their rollercoastering spectacle include: Lake Vyrnwy RSPB, Powys; Acres Down, Hampshire (see New Forest); Haldon Forest, Devon; New Fancy View in the Forest of Dean, Gloucestershire; and Wykeham Forest, Yorkshire.

11. GROUSE

Grouse are surely among the most British of birds. They are attractive, charismatic, even eccentric. We tend to take them a bit for granted or even see them in a negative light (with regards to Hen Harriers, for instance), however they are a fascinating group of species, each with its own curious display strategies. It wasn't so long ago that grouse could be found throughout the UK, but over the past century the population of Black Grouse has declined massively with a loss of range covering the entire southern half of Britain. Red Grouse has also contracted its range and Capercaillie is now extinct from many of its former haunts, with its core range centred on the Spey Valley. Ptarmigan still persist throughout most of their former range but are generally under-recorded.

When making the effort to see grouse displaying most people tend to visit a Black Grouse lek, or maybe the Capercaillie viewpoint at Loch Garten, yet how often have you gone out to enjoy Red Grouse displaying or really pushed it and found displaying Ptarmigan? Both Black Grouse and Capercaillie are stunning and highly entertaining when in their full pomp, with fizzing, bubbling, popping, strutting and fighting – there isn't much that doesn't happen at a lek! They can provide hours of entertainment and enjoyment for the observer.

Much like Black Grouse, Red Grouse are most active at dawn and dusk and in areas with a high density of birds the moors can come alive with their *go-back go-back go-back* calls, and males erupting vertically out of the heather into the air as they signal their prowess and defend their territories. The action of one male displaying often elicits a response from its neighbours and before long the whole moor can be bursting with grouse catapulting themselves skyward. They are very much the essence of British moors; an endemic taxa and charismatic species that by fate has been managed for sport, thus maintaining both high population densities and the typically more transitional moorland habitat upon which they occur.

Ptarmigan are inhabitants of our high tops, where the landscapes are dominated by lichens, heathy tundra, rocky plateaus and scree. They are our hardiest bird species, rarely descending to altitudes lower than 2,300ft (700m)

Above: Making any effort to see Ptarmigan is worthwhile but dawn forays onto the high slopes provide a unique insight into the lives of these enigmatic grouse.

Opposite: Black Grouse leks are the most commonly visited by birders, but all grouse species display in some form or other.

Following spread: A male Capercaillie leks in Scotland.

and frequently enduring day after day of sub-zero temperatures. Their display is not as extravagant as those of the other grouse species but it is by no means less interesting. A series of creaking, snoring, belching and popping notes resonate from invisible beings. If the bird remains static it is often nigh on impossible to locate, however the birds can produce these bizarre notes in a song flight which may end with a plummeting descent down the flanks of a Munro on bowed stiff white wings.

WHEN AND WHERE

Grouse are easily disturbed. To witness displays you need to be up before the lark and in position before the grouse arrive on their lek (for lekking species). The best option for seeing Black Grouse and Capercaillie is to join a guided walk, or visit a recognised viewing site, but if you wish to find your own lek, using your car as a hide is often the most comfortable and least obtrusive way of watching the birds. Ptarmigan nearly always require a walk-in to get to the best sites. These are high and potentially dangerous areas so please make sure you are fully equipped to deal with anything the mountains may throw at you.

Almost all grouse start to become territorial as soon as the days start getting longer. Red Grouse and Ptarmigan can be particularly vocal from January through until April, while Black Grouse will lek from February until early June, and displaying Capercaillie are best witnessed in April and May.

Red Grouse are common and widespread in Scotland, northern England and North Wales, with smaller populations in higher hills of South Wales and Dartmoor. Red Grouse may be frequently observed from the roadside in many of these areas. Ptarmigan are confined the Scottish Highlands, generally in locations above 2,300ft (700m). The most easily accessed sites are the radar station just east of Applecross Bay, Sutherland, Cairngorm Ski Centre, and the Cobbler, an easily accessible mountain at the north end of Loch Long. Black Grouse may still be located in North Wales with great viewing at the Llandegla Forest Centre, Denbighshire. They are also scattered in the Peak District and Pennines although most leks are not easily viewable. Langdon Beck in Upper Teesdale, Durham, is a reliable lek site that can be viewed from the car. In Scotland the species is still relatively widespread but generally scarce. The most accessible leks are in Abernethy Forest, Galloway Forest Park, Glen Cluaine, the eastern Cairngorms, and around Loch Awe where birds may be viewed from the roadside (none of the these Scottish sites are included within the gazetteer).

12. NEST FINDING

There is something innate and natural for many of us about wanting to find birds' nests. An inquisitive, almost hunter-gather instinct and a child-like fascination with the construction and development of the nest, the eggs, its chicks and the fledging. Not so long ago many children and adults partook in this pastime, some for fun, while others for the more harmful fascination of collecting clutches. This pursuit is now thankfully illegal.

Nests are amazing structures. They are designed to hold and protect, insulate and conceal the eggs and chicks. Some can hardly be described as nests at all, for instance the narrow ledges on which Guillemots breed, teetering precariously hundreds of feet above the thunderous ocean. Others are the pinnacle of concealment, with the Wren's nest being a classic example; beautifully domed and embedded into its surroundings, often within the complex root-ball of a fallen tree or perfectly placed into the end of a disused pipe. Other nests, such as that of the Long-tailed Tit, are delicately made of lichen and built into the tangles of thorny bushes, while Goldcrests create such dainty structures that spiders' webs are

used to weave the component items together. Maybe in due course we will see Penduline Tits breeding in the UK – this is a species that binds together the seeds of bulrushes to create a pendulous (hence the name) nest with a long hanging entrance tunnel, normally suspended from willows overhanging water.

There is always a sense of joy associated with discovering a nest. Maybe it's a sense of achievement or an innocent delight at the vulnerability of the contents, or the feeling that for just a moment you have a window into a whole other world. In some cases the sense of surprise and achievement in the observer is magnified by the elusiveness and scarcity of the species, for instance discovering a Grasshopper Warbler nest when the female leaps from the clump of sedge and scuttles, mouse-like,

Above: Nests and their contents are always exciting discoveries. This is a Song Thrush nest.

Opposite: A typical Blackbird nest with eggs and a chick.

Following spread: A Reed Warbler's nest is a beautifully intricate structure.

away through the vegetation to try and avoid detection.

Of course if you don't want to go searching for nests then it is easy enough to bring the birds to you. Why not try creating new nest sites for species that may not breed in your garden such as Swift, House Martin, Tawny Owl, Barn Owl and Spotted Flycatcher, or even expand the possibilities for tits and robins to breed. You can even get boxes with built-in cameras linked directly to your computer so there's no need to disturb the breeding birds.

WHEN AND WHERE

Birds can be found breeding in every month of the year. From Crossbills and Cormorants in January to Woodpigeons and Great Crested Grebes in November and December and every month in between. The peak months for breeding activity are April to July.

Unsurprisingly nests can be found anywhere and everywhere. Some of our more ubiquitous species such as Robin, Blackbird and Collared Dove may be found in just about any garden with sufficient cover to support a nest. Many species, such as Swallow and Wren, take advantage of open outbuildings, while others, including Spotted Flycatcher, Redstart and House Martin, will use the exteriors, cracks and crevices of buildings. A search of almost any habitat is spring is likely to result in the discovery of a nest. The best method other than cold-searching is to sit and watch an area from a distance and wait for adults returning with food. A careful approach to the area often results in a nest being located.

GET INVOLVED

The BTO has been running the Nest Record Scheme (NRS) for over 75 years. To date more than 1.25 million nest records of 232 species have been submitted, with each one detailing the location, number of eggs and chicks, and the outcome of each nest. These data, collected by members of the public, have built a vast and thorough knowledge of our species' breeding patterns and have enabled trends to be identified.

Breeding birds and nests should always be treated with as much care and respect as possible. Many are prone to disturbance and prolonged visits, touching and removing eggs and chicks may cause birds to desert a nest. In addition some species are also protected by law and require a license in order to visit the breeding site. Please consult the BTO and NRS website for further information.

13. SKYLARKS

Frequently the Skylark appears to us as nothing more than a sandy-brown bird, possibly even a dull bird, generally seen scratting around among loose soil for seeds, crouching furtively to avoid detection. Yet its song is one of the most recognisable of all British birds and instantly evokes a sense of place, of open British landscapes, farmland, moors, dunes or downs.

Over the past 40 years the Skylark population has declined by over 75 per cent, yet it is still a widespread species which is common in places. Its decline is widely attributed to agricultural intensification and a change in farming activities to autumn-sown cereals, as well as to the removal of field margins, the ploughing of winter stubbles and the increased use of pesticides. Recent trials by the RSPB have shown that farming in a more sympathetic way is enough to boost local populations of not only Skylark but also other charismatic species such as Grey Partridge, Yellowhammer and Tree Sparrow. In many ways the Skylark has become a vanguard for all farmland birds challenged by our ever intensifying and industrialised methods of managing the land. It is fascinating to think that before humans arrived in the UK the sounds of the Skylark would most likely have been limited to pockets of naturally open habitat in a land otherwise blanketed by wildwood, and it was only the conversion of this land to agriculture that enabled the Skylark to spread. It is therefore rather ironic that a song so inherently linked to our agricultural landscape is now declining as a result of pressures created by humans.

Whether you step out before dawn in spring, during the height of the midday sun in mid-summer, or as the sun sets on the solstice, there is a chance you will hear Skylarks. Whilst the peak singing activity occurs once the sun has risen and for the first few hours of the day, many birds will continue to sing throughout the day and some can even occasionally be heard singing from high above you in the heavy darkness of the early hours. In the twilight hours the air is still and cool, sound travels far better than later in the day, and this is when the articulation of every note is apparent and the complexity, whimsicality and sheer perfection of delivery becomes crystal clear.

How many times have you stopped to look for a singing Skylark? On those beautiful sunny days when the sky is deep ocean-blue and you lay back in the grass, it can often take a while to pick out the tiny male Skylark high above you singing note after note after note on ever-flapping wings. There is something profoundly relaxing and very British about being able to close your eyes, feel the sun's warmth on your skin, inhale the fresh scents of summer flowers or heather, and listen to the gentle hum of insects under the shower of eloquent and varied Skylark notes. With the recent evidence that, unsurprisingly, enjoying a good view or a beautiful outdoor experience alleviates stress and tension, maybe we should be investing even more effort and funding into the conservation of species such as the Skylark and landscapes such as low-intensity farmland, in order to reap more of the benefits of their therapeutic properties as well as their conservation and intrinsic values.

WHEN AND WHERE

Skylarks can still be found throughout the UK in any open grassy or arable habitat, as well as on sand-dune systems and in upland areas, especially in places where moorland meets upland pasture. Whilst these birds tend to flock together during the winter months they start returning to breeding areas from March, when the first song can be heard. Males will continue to sing through spring and into summer. The best time to hear them is for the first four hours after the sun has risen, although they may sing throughout the day and even pre-dawn and post-dusk.

Page 75: Skylarks will sing from the ground as well as in flight.

Above: Skylarks often shelter in areas of long grass or crops.

Opposite: How often have you strained your eyes trying to detect a singing Skylark high above you?

14. SPRING SKUA PASSAGE

Skuas are awesome birds – sleek, powerful, ruthless, and masters of piracy on the high seas. Only Arctic and Great Skuas (see 23. Bonxies) breed in the UK but come spring and autumn both Pomarine and Long-tailed Skuas also journey along our coasts between Arctic breeding grounds and Southern-Hemisphere wintering grounds. Unless you make a trip to northern Scotland in summer, experiences of these birds are generally from windswept headlands as they power past, often far out to sea (see chapter 31, Seawatching).

There is however a spectacle that occurs in spring which is well worth the effort to see. Long-tailed Skuas are the most dainty, elegant and attractive member of the family. They have neat, attenuated bodies with deep chests, tail streamers that whip in the wind, slick cocoa-black caps, and rich butter-toned cheeks and breasts all creating a perfectly coloured and proportioned bird. Long-tailed Skuas are remarkable in their north-bound migration. As they head north from Antarctic and southern Atlantic waters they follow the western edge of the Atlantic, along the eastern seaboard of the States and out to the Grand Banks off Canada, from where they fly due east across the Atlantic towards the UK before banking north-east and heading up to their breeding grounds in Scandinavia. What's more the majority of this breeding population moves during the course of a two-week period between the middle and the end of May. If the conditions are just right this movement of birds can be displaced onto the British coast in spectacular style. The displacement requires strong north-westerly winds over a period of days to push the migrating skua flocks in from the open ocean and onto our coasts. In some places flocks of hundreds of Long-tailed Skuas can be seen powering their way along the coast.

And it's not just along the open coast where they occur. The narrowing sea lochs of the Scottish west coast funnel the skuas and encourage them to make impressive overland movements across Scotland to the North Sea, where they continue their migration in a north-easterly direction. Seeing any skua heading inland is a fantastic sight, but to witness flock after flock of Long-tailed Skuas, often intermingled with skuas of the other three

species, is something else. At the head of the lochs, the skuas circle up, calling, slowly gaining height against the impressive backdrop of highland peaks before reaching their desired cruising height where they level off and advance inland through the glens, passing unseen until they are out the other side.

Of course the three other species also make impressive movements and Pomarine Skuas especially can be seen in very large numbers in similar locations to Long-tailed Skuas. They also appear in good numbers further south, where flocks of striking adults, sometimes including dark-morph birds, can be seen loafing on the sea before making overland crossings.

Above: A visit to North Uist during the month of May offers the opportunity to watch groups of migrating Long-tailed Skuas.

Following spread left: Long-tailed Skua is the most elegant of all the skuas and overland migrations bring them close enough to us to enjoy their beautiful patterning and buoyant energetic flight.

Following spread right: Arctic Skuas, a UK breeder, also migrate overland and at some sites all four skua species can be seen in a day taking the overland shortcut.

WHEN AND WHERE

The spring overland passage can commence from mid-April although the peak time is normally May, before numbers ease off in June. All four species can be seen migrating overland with Arctic and Great Skuas occurring throughout this time frame while Pomarine Skuas tend to migrate more in May and June and Long-tailed Skuas peak between 18–31 May.

The most reliable location for witnessing the spring Long-tailed Skua passage is Aird an Runair on North Uist, Outer Hebrides. Here birds cut over the northern corner of the island and into The Minch. Saltcoats Harbour on the Ayrshire coast is also an excellent and reliable spot for witnessing skuas moving inland, and for the majority of people it is more easily accessible than the Western Isles. The Corran Ferry in the Great Glen can see birds moving inland (occasionally in spectacular numbers) backed by impressive scenery, and Fort George in the Moray Firth is a good spot to see them descending to the sea after their land-crossing. Noup Head, Westray, Orkney has also recently proved to be a great spot for witnessing Long-tailed Skuas migrating. Other sites that are good for all skuas include the Solway viaduct, Cumbria; Criccieth Beach, Gwynedd; Dungeness (good for Pomarine Skuas), Kent; and Portland Bill, Dorset. Hound Point in the Firth of Forth can be good for a return overland passage of skuas in the autumn.

15. DAWN CHORUS

The dawn chorus is one of nature's most beautiful experiences. At the most basic of levels it is a joy to listen to. To the trained ear a good dawn chorus is the most complex symphony performed by the best orchestra in the world with multiple pieces of music all playing simultaneously in apparent perfect harmony. It's breathtaking. If however you have an untrained ear, and your aim is to identify the origins of every sound, then listening to the dawn chorus can be a bit like being thrown into a bustling market square where everyone speaks a different language, none of which you can understand.

Bird song is like language. It takes time and effort to learn, as was pointed out in chapter 6 (Bird Sounds). The more we learn the more we appreciate and enjoy what we are listening to and the more we can read into the environment around us without using our eyes. In fact closing your eyes while listening to any bird sound heightens the experience by restricting visual stimuli and channelling aural stimuli.

The dawn chorus is a critical part of the day (and year) for birds, especially

males. It serves to advertise an individual's prowess as a potential suitor through its song skills and helps to delineate territories. Males will endeavour to maintain a territory fit for rearing offspring through vocal communications rather than aggression. The latter is energetic and physically more costly and can occasionally even result in loss of life. The majority of species that join the dawn chorus are insectivorous and singing at the beginning of the day has two very important benefits: firstly sound travels much better through cold and still air (dawn is generally the coolest and calmest part of the day), and secondly the activity levels of insects tend to be lowest then, so substituting foraging with singing does not prove as energetically costly as it would do later in the

Above: The Nightingale is the ultimate songster and well worth getting up early to hear.

Opposite: The Song Thrush is typically one of the first songsters of the day. Its song can be distinguished from that of the Blackbird by its repeated notes.

Following page: Male Chaffinch in full song. One of our most common birds, but frequently ignored because it is so ubiquitous.

day. Species that have adapted to life in dense woodlands have evolved their songs accordingly. With so many large and solid objects around them, the songs and notes they produce need to travel the furthest distance possible without being distorted, and to this end you will notice that many woodland species produce clearer and longer notes, often whistles – for example those of thrushes, Nightingale, Blackcap and Chaffinch. In comparison those species from more open and scrubby habitats, such as whitethroats and Linnet have more varied, jangly and scratchy songs as the sounds are less distorted by structures around them. This also explains why many birds sing from high points.

Learning bird song is a fun and fascinating experience. It provides a deeper understanding of what is happening around you and occasionally an indirect hint as to which other species may

be present that have thus far eluded your detection. As a further means of attracting a mate many males will incorporate snippets of a different species' song or call into their own song. This mimicry diversifies the song and advertises the male as being of a better pedigree. Whilst most examples of mimicry involve common species occasionally something more unusual will be incorporated, for instance summer migrants seem to have a preference for adding snatches of Bee-eater call into the repertoire, and Starlings will add just about anything from Fulmar and terns to Rustic Bunting and Osprey.

Whether you enjoy the dawn chorus for its simple natural beauty or for the complexity of species, songs, mimicry and adaptation, it is an experience that is well worth getting up early for.

WHEN AND WHERE

The dawn chorus may be experienced anywhere although the best locations are generally woodlands, with mature and mixed forests generally harbouring the highest diversity of species. Marshes can also produce a stunning variety of bird song (see chapter 22), and even urban environments can have in excess of 20 species singing at dawn. In general the first songsters become active in early January, and these can include Song and Mistle Thrushes, Great Tit and Woodpigeon. The list of songsters gradually increases as spring progresses with a noticeable surge in numbers and species as summer migrants return to a blossoming spring. A peak in diversity and intensity is reached around mid-May before bird song starts to decline and becomes almost absent by July. To maximise your enjoyment of the dawn chorus you really need to be out from about half an hour before sunrise. Places such as Blean Woods, Kent, Minsmere, Suffolk, Highnam Woods, Gloucestershire, and Brampton Woods, Cambridgeshire, all offer great dawn chorus experiences and even the chance of encountering a Nightingale. Sites such as Wildboarclough, Cheshire, and Goyt Valley, Derbyshire, are great places to enjoy a huge range of species at dawn. If you're lucky and you get up early enough a dawn chorus walk may also yield roding Woodcock (chapter 9) or churring Nightjars (chapter 21).

GET INVOLVED

Many reserves with suitable habitat offer dawn chorus events. These are a brilliant way to experience bird song and if you are new to birding then a helping hand deciphering the different songs can be especially useful. Check local reserve websites for more detail.

16. OAK WOODLAND BIRDING

The Atlantic seaboard of Europe supports a unique habitat of which the UK hosts the vast majority. Thriving oak woods cling to the moisture-laden valleys of Wales, south-west England, the Lake District and western Scotland. In many cases these are the remnants of original wildwood, habitats almost unchanged for thousands of years and which once would have enveloped the rest of the UK in one form or another. They are stunning places to visit. Gnarled, ancient trees naturally stunted by wind, salt and shallow soils. The trunks are carpeted in velvety green moss and the limbs are festooned with lichens, liverworts and ferns. The spring awakening in these valley is often a tardy one, and its not until mid-May that a burst of vibrant green brings the trees back to life, coinciding with a sea of blue beneath as the bluebells bloom.

Similarly the birdlife in these valleys is often late to start compared with other woodland areas. The woods come alive with the arrival of spring migrants from the south. While Blackcaps, Chiffchaffs and Willow Warblers are often the forerunners, the main arrival occurs in mid- to late April when Pied Flycatchers and Redstarts flood back into the canopies. Wood Warblers arrive shortly after, and finally Spotted

Flycatchers in early to mid-May. The songs of flycatchers, Redstarts and Wood Warblers resonate through the woods, proclaiming the arrival of spring. Trying to see these songsters can be an altogether different matter. Fleeting glimpses of colour and contrast allude to the presence of these trans-Saharan migrants, and tantalise the observer. We don't automatically think of woodlands as being bright and colourful places, but with red, blue, yellow, black, white and vivid-green plumages and bright green foliage it's hard to deny that these oak woods are anything but. Just occasionally a line of sight through the mosaic of leaves and branches provides a clear view of a singing male Pied Flycatcher or Redstart perched in the canopy – when it happens it's a moment worth savouring.

As with the song of the Skylark (see chapter 13), you can

Above: The Redstart is an icon of oak woodland birds.

Opposite: A classic spring oak woodland complete with a carpet of bluebells.

Following spread: The trill of Wood Warblers high in the canopy rounds off a perfect May morning in an oak woodland.

achieve a sense of place simply by listening to the landscape of sounds around you. Where else in the UK would deliver Wood Warbler, Pied Flycatcher, Redstart and potentially Red Kite and Goshawk? The rich earthy smells and the fresh clean air are also features that stimulate the senses and allude to the location.

As soon as these migrants arrive back they get to work proclaiming and defending territories and suitable nesting holes. Wood Warblers commence building intricate doomed nests among the winter-worn grass clumps beneath the oaks and Spotted Flycatchers line nooks and crevices within contorted trunks and branches. At the base of these oak woods run fast-flowing streams that are a product of the steep-sided valleys. Frequenting these dark and dank streams Dippers and Grey Wagtails bounce and bob from rock to rock.

The more remote woodlands can be home to some of our most elusive raptors as well, including Goshawk and Honey Buzzard. Both prefer undisturbed mature forests where they can hunt for prey or forage for wasp and bee nests. Nowadays the Red Kite is becoming an increasingly common sight but in the not-too-distant past, at its lowest ebb, the last few pairs in Britain were confined to the quiet Welsh oak woods.

Of course many common species also inhabit these woodlands, from tits and thrushes to Chaffinches, Treecreepers, Nuthatches and in some areas Lesser Spotted Woodpeckers and Hawfinches. Paying a visit to this habitat at dawn not only maximises your enjoyment of the place and the experience, but also offers the chance to experience the dawn chorus (see chapter 15) and practice your bird sound identification (see chapter 6).

WHEN AND WHERE

The last week of April through to the last week in May see the peak in bird activity in these oak woods – this is a frenzied period of breeding and song. Activity levels are still high in June although by then many birds have finished singing. These woodlands are best visited in the first few hours of the day.

There are many fine examples of oak woodlands, however some of the best and most easily accessible include: Devil's Bridge, Ceredigion; Lake Vyrnwy, Powys; Aber Valley, Gwynedd; Strid Wood, Yorkshire; Wood of Cree, Dumfries and Galloway; Killiecrankie, Perthshire; and Taynish NNR, Argyll.

17. CUCKOOS

The Cuckoo's song is undoubtedly the most instantly recognisable of all British birds. It is a natural alarm clock, a seasonal beacon, and a conservation hero. The Cuckoo has been championed by writers and poets for centuries, but sadly it is currently in the limelight for all the wrong reasons – a nationwide decline.

Once widespread across the UK, the Cuckoo has suffered a 65 per cent decline since the 1980s, with lowland populations faring particularly badly. The BTO has undertaken a huge amount of research investigating the relationship between the Cuckoo and its host species, which include Meadow Pipit, Pied Wagtail, Dunnock and Reed Warbler, and although there has been a shift in the breeding times of some of these species, it is not enough to explain such a huge decline. It seems likely

that changes in prey availability (caterpillars), or changes elsewhere on their migration route or wintering grounds are having a more significant impact.

The name 'Cuckoo' is onomatopoeic, that is the name sounds like the sound the bird makes, with Chiffchaff, Corncrake (the scientific name, *Crex crex*) and Chough being other examples. The *koog-gooo* song rings out before daylight and can be heard at any time of day; it is always a welcome sound for birders. Often singing from

Above: After an epic trans-saharan journey many birds will spend just a few short weeks in the UK before commencing their journey south again, some having departed by early June.

Opposite: There is nothing more evocative than the song of the Cuckoo.

the tops of trees, these highly territorial males will rapidly respond to a human impersonator – try cupping your hands and blowing through your thumbs as if making an owl hoot, but open and close the gap between your thumbs to create a tonal difference, exhale more rapidly to begin with to get the *koog*, slowing to give a more drawn-out *gooo.* The song is a key symbol of changing seasons, an evocator of fine spring mornings and a joy to listen to and watch.

Not only is hearing and seeing Cuckoos a brilliant experience, especially males in spring, but finding a nest in which a female is laying is something else. This can be done by careful observation of female Cuckoos or by chance. I can still vividly remember one hot May day 10 years ago. I had been surveying an area of upland forestry plantation and moorland in Mid Wales. The woodland held Crossbills, Tree Pipits and Black Grouse, while the rides teemed with Meadow Pipits, and of course there were Cuckoos. Like clockwork they would call the day in and sing the day out. The sky was clear and blue and the day particularly hot. The survey was coming to an end and

as I strolled along the final heathery forest ride a Meadow Pipit flew out from under my feet giving alarm calls. Surely this was a nest. I approached the slight hummock sprawled with rank heather and lifted the branches. The perfectly cup-shaped nest of a Meadow Pipit hugged an egg and a chick but something was wrong – an egg teetered on the rim and another chick lay motionless just beneath. A flush of realisation hit me that this was a Cuckoo chick! I watched for only a few seconds as the minutes' old chick wrestled with the remaining egg, forcing it up the wall of the nest and out over the rim to certain death. I quickly took a photo, gently lowered the cloak of heather boughs, and backed away into the dry warmth of the ride. The excitement of the discovery electrified me and I couldn't wait to get back to the site two weeks later. Fourteen days seemed like an eternity. My route mirrored my previous survey transect. I arrived back at the hummock. The air, normally abuzz with Meadow Pipit alarm calls, was silent. Apprehension overwhelmed me. I slowly lifted the heather bow and there to my delight was a plump, fully feathered Cuckoo chick with a tango-orange gape fully open and pointed in my direction. This little fella was not happy to see me. Once again I was overcome with an immense sense of joy for the bird, awe for the surrogate parents, and trepidation for what awaited the chick over the next few weeks of its life.

WHEN AND WHERE

Cuckoos typically arrive back around mid-April in southern England, and a little later further north, with many Scottish birds appearing in May. The males advertise their presence from the tops of trees, fence posts and outcrops. Singing often starts pre-dawn and the birds are most vociferous for the first few hours of daylight and again towards dusk. Upland populations seem to have fared better than those in the lowlands and the edges of conifer plantations are often favoured locations for Cuckoos.

GETTING INVOLVED

The BTO tracking project has been a great success and is one which you can support. Find out more about the phenomenal movements of Cuckoos that breed in Britain at: www.bto.org/science/migration/tracking-studies/cuckoo-tracking

A similar study on Cuckoos in China has also uncovered some mind-boggling results and can be viewed at: https://birdingbeijing.com/beijing-cuckoo-project/

18. SPRING WADERS

As the days lengthen and the temperatures rise, the swarms of winter waders, triggered by these changes, start to break up and commence their journeys back north to their breeding grounds. From drab winter plumages the environmental cues stimulate a moult – the loss of one set of feathers and the growth of an entirely new set (see chapter 4, Feathers). Now the birds have drive and purpose. For many the summer season at higher latitudes is a short one and the birds need to arrive, attract a mate, lay eggs, rear young and depart south again before the return of long dark nights and freezing conditions. To maximise the chances of attracting a mate or remaining camouflaged our drab winter shorebirds acquire often stunning breeding plumages. Against a plain sandy beach or muddy estuary they stand out like bright flecks of paint speckled across the shore, yet on territory in the Arctic tundra they blend in perfectly. Russet, maroon, black and white disrupt the outline of the bird and an incubating female becomes almost invisible against the collage of bright tundra vegetation.

Flocks are frequently small but can be mixed, with Dunlin, Turnstone and Ringed Plover making a beautifully contrasting mix of colours, plumages and of course

feeding actions. Many flocks leave the large mudflats of their wintering grounds and can be found in smaller bays and on open beaches, as well as on gravel pits and lake edges.

The later in the spring you encounter birds the more likely they are to be in fine summer attire. You may notice that in April and early May, many birds appear to have a pale cast to the plumage. This is down to tiny pale tips to an otherwise brightly coloured feather. Pale pigments are weaker than darker pigments and as a result they slowly abrade down revealing the bolder colours underneath. At some locations, especially along the East Anglian coast, it may be possible to see 20 species of waders in a day in May. Here in the brackish and freshwater lagoons chequered Grey Plovers jostle for position alongside brick-red Black-tailed Godwits

Above: Breeding-plumaged male Ruff aren't so much the kings of spring waders as the jesters – they are eccentric, effervescent and brightly coloured.

Opposite: The sighting of a brick-red breeding-plumaged Black-tailed Godwit will enrich any spring birding day.

Following spread left: The Knot's orange-red breeding plumage contrasts starkly with its dull grey winter plumage.

Following spread right: A Grey Plover with full black face, breast and belly is a striking bird.

and Knot, while maroon-coloured Curlew Sandpipers bicker with rufous, black, white and grey Dunlins. Even species such as Oystercatcher look immaculate with glowing carrot-coloured bills and crisp black and white plumage.

Undoubtedly one of the most eye-catching spring waders is the Ruff. The males transform from a drab grey-brown bird in winter into the most resplendent and eccentric of waders on the planet, all in preparation to dance for the right to mate with the females. The bare facial skin becomes vividly coloured while the ornamental head and neck feathering, the ruff, becomes flared. Even the 'duller' scapulars, mantle and tertials are still beautifully marked with subtle colours tiger-striped and chevroned over them. Ruff breed in northern and eastern Europe where they form leks – areas where multiple males gather to show off their prowess in a series of dances, stand-offs, leaps and runs. The aristocratic feathering exaggerates these displays and the most vigorous male is generally afforded the chance to mate with the most females. Sadly Ruff is a very rare breeding bird in the UK, however they still occur in spring splendour on passage with areas of eastern England and northern Scotland offering the best chance of seeing these amazing birds.

WHEN AND WHERE

The northbound migration occurs from April to early June with shorebirds looking at their best in May and June. You can witness the passage of bright summer-plumaged waders almost anywhere but certain places can hold a phenomenal number of species or provide amazing viewing conditions. These include: Titchwell and Snettisham RSPB and Cley NWT on the Norfolk coast; Minsmere RSPB on the Suffolk coast; Rutland Water; Blacktoft Sands RSPB, Lincolnshire; Goldcliffe Pools, Gwent; Conwy RSPB, Conwy; Marshside RSPB, Merseyside; Musselburgh Lagoon, Lothian; Ythan Estuary, Aberdeenshire; Dornoch beach, Sutherland; and Dunnet Bay and St John's Pool, Caithness.

19. DISPLAYING DUCKS

Nowhere else in the birding world is there such a brilliant spectacle that gets so overlooked. Late winter and early spring see every pond, marsh, lake, reservoir, estuary, bay, in fact anywhere with water, turn into a dance floor. Ducks, 1.8 million of them, spend the winter in the UK. They come from all over – Wigeon from central Russia, Pintail from Scandinavia, Long-tailed Duck from the Arctic tundra, and many more from much closer to home. Some travel 3,000 miles (4,800km) one way to spend the winter in our wetlands. Our marshes and lakes offer relatively mild conditions compared to the particularly harsh climates enveloping the breeding grounds of these ducks during winter.

Wildfowl can be enjoyed on nature reserves, as well as at unprotected sites, from the very northern tip of Scotland to the southern extremities of England. Most frequently we scan through feeding flocks of common duck in search of something slightly more interesting, however the common species can provide just as much pleasure. Duck display is brilliant; it's flamboyant and energetic. The males

of almost all species are a joy to look at when just sitting stationary but add quirky actions and sounds and a common species becomes enigmatic and eccentric. Drake Teal pirouette around each other like whirligig beetles, crowns plumped, tails stuck up, head popping, and all the time giving *bleep* calls. With an energetic thrust they force their bodies upwards into the air almost like a stallion rearing up (or maybe more of a Shetland pony), before quickly dropping back down into the water. Drake Long-tailed Ducks have similar actions but hold their needle-like tail bolt upright while chasing females around sheltered bays, all the time uttering their distinctive crowing call which sounds somewhere between an auk and a gull. Most species become frenzied during

Above: As spring approaches groups of duck such as these Pintail can become highly excitable.

Opposite: A drake Goldeneye in full eccentric display.

Following page: The striking Long-tailed Duck is one of the highlights of a trip to northern Britain in winter.

the course of the display with multiple males joining in and attracting a horde of inquisitive females.

First prize in the display category most definitely goes to the Goldeneye. The males pull out all the stops to win the attention of the females. Groups of males come together with the energy and vibrancy of a Latin dance school. Already smart in their piebald plumage the males twirl around on the water, puffing out their head feathers, and simultaneously throwing back their heads, bringing their wings forward and up, and kicking backwards vigorously with bright orange feet over the surface of the water in such a way to cause a splash.

Duck display is without a doubt one of the highlights of late winter birding and can be encountered almost anywhere where there are decent numbers of ducks. I thoroughly recommend enjoying this brilliant behaviour that is exhibited by many of our common species.

WHEN AND WHERE

While wildfowl are present throughout the year in the UK, numbers are supplemented by birds from the continent during the winter, and the spectacle of duck display is best observed between January and late March. Display is often most intense and most easily seen first thing in the morning of cold, clear days.

Duck display can be seen wherever there are ducks. The best experiences are in locations which allow close approach to wildfowl and ideally even allow the sounds to be heard and these can include town and village ponds and city park lakes such as The Serpentine in Hyde Park, London, Hogganfield Loch, Glasgow, and the Peedie Sea, Kirkwall (a great site for urban Long-tailed Ducks), as well as more traditional locations such as: Slimbridge, Gloucestershire; Martin Mere, Lancashire; Buckenham Marshes, Norfolk; Leighton Moss, Lancashire; and The Loons, Orkney. Coastal and seaduck can be harder to see well although there are a few locations where these birds come close enough to even hear their displays including: Thurso Bay, Caithness; Blackdog, Aberdeenshire; Musselburgh, Lothian; Loch Indaal, Islay, Argyll; and occasionally sites such as Holkham beach, Norfolk, if tidal conditions permit.

SUMMER

A raft of Guillemots on the sea at the base of their breeding cliff.

20. SEABIRD COLONIES

If you've never visited a seabird city then this is a must. They are simply astonishing. An incomprehensible melee of activity, toing and froing, bickering, squabbling, breeding, feeding, life and death. These colonies generally consist of multiple species. On the high sea cliffs Guillemots, Razorbills, Kittiwakes, Fulmars and Gannets jostle to find a suitable breeding ledge or crevice. Where there is more vegetation, normally at the top of the cliff, Puffins burrow into the soil and gulls breed between them. Right at the bottom Shags will often breed on ledges licked by the surging swells. On coastal lagoons and islands gulls and terns dominate. Terns prefer low-lying islands and shingly substrate on which to breed and colonies can contain a mix of several species, with Sandwich, Common and Arctic often all occurring together, and they will frequently mix with smaller gulls as well. Much of the fun of these places is watching the interactions between individuals and species.

Seabird colonies tend to provide a full-on assault on the senses of sight, sound and smell. So many birds together produce large amounts of guano and you can often smell seabirds before you see or even hear them. The chances are that if you visit a colony such as the Farne Islands

you will also depart with some added decoration. Arctic Terns especially can also be quite aggressive towards human intruders and they are well known for dive-bombing folk. It can seem quite intimidating and birds will occasionally draw blood so its always best to either walk close to someone taller than you, or if you happen to be the tallest, place your arm or a stick above your head.

These colonies are massively important in the birds' life history. It is for only this short period each year that they venture on to land (only just in some cases) and the cliff or colony needs to be sufficiently close to rich feeding grounds to enable the adults to commute back and forth. The cliffs, islands and lagoons also need to be safe enough from predators although few colonies are without a marauding aerial foe such as a Great Black-backed Gull, Bonxie or Peregrine, or even a White-tailed Eagle in some places. Many individuals of these seabird species can live in excess of 20 years and often a pair will raise just a single chick each year.

Above: To the untrained eye organised chaos appears to reign in a tern colony. They tend to be incredibly noisy places!

Opposite: There are very few accessible Gannet colonies around the British coast, but sites such as Bempton Cliffs offer the chance to see these birds up close.

Following page: Puffins are one of the most instantly recognisable birds in Britain and are easily seen at many seabird colonies around the country.

Britain is an exceptionally important breeding area for seabirds with millions returning every summer. Auks come from all over the north-east Atlantic to breed on our shores. For most of the year they are masters of the ocean, living and thriving in one of the most extreme environments on the planet. In February 2013 the largest wave ever recorded on the planet occurred just north-west of St Kilda and measured a whopping 19m (62ft). This location is slap-bang in the middle of a key wintering area for Puffins and other auks. I'm not sure which is more impressive, the huge waves or the ability of tiny birds to survive in them?

Most Gannets head south for the winter, spending the harsher months off the coasts of Morocco or Iberia. Our terns however undertake monumental migrations, with Arctic Terns spending the winter in the Southern Ocean, some on the edge of Antarctic ice shelves, while some Sandwich Terns will head to the southern tip of Africa and around the Cape of Good Hope into the Indian Ocean.

WHEN AND WHERE

Seabird colonies are at their most active between May and the beginning of August. Gannet colonies are active from February onwards through until September.

We are fortunate to have many colonies all along our coasts (although breeding auks and Gannets are absent from south-east England) and there is a large amount of information available on the internet. Some of the most accessible sites include: Bempton Cliffs, Yorkshire; Troup Head, Fowlsheugh, and Bullers of Buchan, Aberdeenshire; South Stack, Anglesey; Dunnet Head, Caithness; and Sumburgh Head, Shetland. If you want more of an adventure why not head out to one of our many islands? Among the best are: Lundy Island, Devon; Skomer, Pembrokeshire; Farne Islands, Northumberland; Isle of May, Fife; Handa Island, Sutherland; and St Kilda, Highland.

Tern colonies are widely scattered around our coast, with some occurring at the sites listed above. Elsewhere good locations include: Langstone Harbour, Hampshire; Brownsea Island, Dorset; Dungeness, Kent; Minsmere, Suffolk; Blakeney Point, Norfolk; Cemlyn Bay, Anglesey; St John's Pool, Caithness; and Forvie, Aberdeenshire.

For something completely different why not visit the urban Kittiwake colonies in Gateshead, Newcastle, including a specially constructed Kittiwake Tower.

Colonies can be sensitive to disturbance and you should always remain on marked trails to avoid crushing and killing eggs and chicks, as well as for your own safety. Many sites are also particularly dangerous, being near cliffs.

21. NIGHTJARS

Nightjars have a rich history in the UK. Known also by the traditional names of 'Eve-jarr', 'Goatsucker', and 'Puckeridge' they suffered persecution through a human fear of the unknown. Crepuscular in their habits and cryptic in plumage, people once thought they struck calves in the night and inflicted distemper on them, when in fact this condition was caused by warble flies. Elsewhere people believed that under the cover of darkness Nightjars snuck in to suckle the teats of goats. This myth had been propagated since the days of Aristotle. Now we know that none of this is true and Nightjars are fondly regarded for their association with summer.

Many of us make the effort to see Nightjars soon after they have arrived back on territory, when days are long and warm nights are filled with the scent of heathland flowers, gorse or fresh pine. Many of the places that Nightjars inhabit conjure a tranquil atmosphere in the mind, filled only with natural and soothing sights, sounds and smells.

Seeing a Nightjar in the day is almost impossible. The intricate feather pattern of greys and browns melts their outline into that of their day-roost perch or the mottled ground on which they nest. Their huge glossy black eyes vanish as the eyelids clench tight. It's only after dark that the finer features of the face, including their immensely wide mouth (surrounded by bristles to help guide in insect prey into their beaks), come into play, and our eyes lack the ability to detect these. What we do see is almost ghostly. Against the final glow of the day a bird glides into view jinking left, twisting right. They are silent in flight and exceptionally adept at changing direction in the quickest of motions. An inquisitive species, Nightjars will often approach an observer, hovering close by, occasionally calling in alarm, before melting into the darkness once again.

Nightjars become active soon after the sun sets, when males leave their daytime roosts on the branches of trees and start to advertise their territory and attract a mate. This unique sound, the churring, is perhaps the most charming element of the bird. The 'jar' part of its name derives from 'jarring', that 'harsh, inharmonious sound'. This song can even be likened to the repetitive notes of some insects. When

multiple males start to churr an area can reverberate with the sound of Nightjars, creating quite an atmosphere. The experience of standing, sitting or even lying on a perfect summer's eve, eyes to the stars and a sound track of Nightjars (and likely other species such as Grasshopper Warbler or Nightingale), is not to be missed. For many it is an annual pilgrimage, and I have many fond memories of father-son trips in search of this species in North Wales as a lad. If you have not ventured out in search of these amazing birds then I thoroughly recommend that you make the effort to do so.

Above: Nightjars are notoriously difficult to see during the day but churring males can be more prominent as dusk falls.

Following spread: Beautifully camouflaged, the Nightjar is a cryptic but beautiful summer migrant.

WHEN AND WHERE

Nightjars are one of our last summer migrants to arrive and one of the first to leave. Typically birds are back on territory in mid-May and they become increasingly elusive from mid-August, yet in this time they can raise two broods. The best time to witness the spectacle of Nightjars in action is for two hours from sunset and again for an hour or so leading up to dawn. Peak activity occurs between mid-May and early June and again in early to mid-July. Nightjars are a Schedule 1 breeding species and it is an offence to disturb them during the breeding season. Please do not use playback to elicit a response.

Nightjars prefer open heathland, young or felled conifer plantations and open dry hillsides and can be found from the south coast of England to southern Scotland. There are a number of easily accessible sites which provide the opportunity to see and hear these birds without disturbing them. Observers should always remain on roads, tracks and footpaths where they are unlikely to cause disturbance to breeding birds. Key sites include: Arne RSPB, Dorset; Blean Woods RSPB, Kent; Kelling Heath and Breckland, Norfolk; Cannock Chase, Staffordshire; and Clocaenog Forest, Denbighshire.

22. NOCTURNAL MARSH BIRDING

Nocturnal birding is a brilliant experience, almost like a parallel universe of birding. We take for granted the visual element of birding and often neglect our other faculties, but once the light fades it opens up a whole new world dominated by sound and sometimes even smell (see also: 9. Drumming Snipe and Roding Woodcock; 21. Nightjars; 24. Tubenose colonies; and, to a lesser extent 34. Starling Murmurations and 40. Raven Roosts).

Marshes are dense impenetrable places for us, but for many birds they offer shelter, protection and an abundance of food. They are so dense however that the songs and calls of many species do not travel far enough to advertise their territories effectively and as a result they have to climb to the tops of reed stems to project their voices. This puts them at risk from predators, so when better to advertise yourself than at night? Add to this the all-encompassing silence that often descends on wetlands (and indeed most habitats) at night and you have the perfect arena for making yourself heard.

Come late April, May, and continuing into June, marshes can reverberate with songs and calls. Sedge, Reed and

Grasshopper Warblers dominate the soundscapes in most places, with males blasting intricate songs, stolen notes and melodies out across the marshlands desperately trying to attract a mate. Snipe and other waders such as Redshank can often be heard singing at night, and for crakes and rails this is *the* time to find them, with Water Rails producing an accelerating *kupp kupp kupp* sound, completely unrelated to the pig-like squeals we so often associate with this marsh-dweller. You may even be lucky enough to hear the 'whiplash' song of the Spotted Crake, which can travel as far as 1.25 miles (2km).

Where open water is present the growls, croaks, and quacks of ducks add further layers of sound to the scene. In addition to the standard *quack* calls of Mallards you may hear the 'querquedulations' of Garganey, the *treel*

Above: Spotted Crakes are almost impossible to see in the day but their presence is betrayed after nightfall by a distinctive 'whiplash' call.

Opposite: Marshes come alive at dusk during spring and early summer.

Following page: Grasshopper Warblers make themselves known as the sun goes down.

calls of Teal, the beautiful whistles of Wigeon, or the grunts of Tufted Duck.

The challenge is often in picking out different species from this cacophony of noise. It can be incredibly difficult trying to discern a single species, or endeavouring to identify a distant song or call above other louder songsters. There are a couple of good ways of enhancing your experience. Firstly close your eyes. They are almost useless in the inky blackness of night so why not hone your other senses towards the experience, especially your hearing. Another useful tip is to cup your hands behind your ears so that they amplify the sounds coming from the direction you are facing and reduce the noises from other directions. Try to choose sites that are well away from roads to maximise the enjoyment.

Whilst other habitats can also provide interesting nocturnal soundscapes there is something mesmerising about standing on a bund or causeway overlooking a reedbed. Often mist descends on these areas creating an ethereal feel – the air can be cooler and the earthy smells can be intense, sometimes too intense. It is a sensory overload, with the visuals taking a backseat for a change.

WHEN AND WHERE

You can experience the joys of night birding in marshes at any time of year although without a doubt they are at their most energetic in the early summer months when migrants have returned and breeding activity is at its maximum. Winter months can also prove productive with concentrations of duck and snipe providing an entertaining sound scene.

Please note, marshes can be dangerous places, especially after dark, and you should be familiar with the site before venturing into it at night, and always stay on well marked tracks. Please only visit sites that allow public access after dark as well and let someone know where you're going.

Any accessible marsh is worth listening over, however particular hot-spots include: The Loons RSPB, Orkney; Loch Gruinart RSPB, Islay, Argyll; Moine Mhor, Argyll; Leighton Moss RSPB , Lancashire; Wheldrake Ings YWT, Yorkshire; Norfolk Broads, especially Hickling Broad (where there is an accessible bund to Rush Hills scrape); Cors Bodeilio NNR, Anglesey; Ham Wall RSPB, Somerset; Marazion Marsh RSPB, Cornwall.

23. BONXIES

The Great Skua, or Bonxie as it is known up north, is the ultimate bully of the air, a supreme pirate, afraid of nothing, with nothing to lose and everything to gain. As a species it has gone from strength to strength in Britain with an estimated 60 per cent of a world population of 16,000 breeding territories situated within the UK. The Scottish breeding population has expanded its range south in recent years to the coast of Ireland.

During migration Great Skuas can be encountered along most sections of the British coastline although they are often a considerable distance offshore. They are also occasionally encountered after big winter storms which blow them inshore, where they tend to predate wrecked

seabirds (see 31. Seawatching), and can be seen in small numbers migrating inland along traditional land-crossing points for skuas in April and May (see 14. Spring Skua Passage).

Bonxies are fearsome. They are robust and equipped with a powerful hooked bill and very sharp claws, not to mention speed. Out of all the skuas they are the most formidable. They specialise in kleptoparasitism, piracy to you and I, waiting for other birds to catch their prey then pursuing them at speed until they are forced to

Above: A pair of Great Skuas, or Bonxies.

Opposite: An incoming Bonxie is a formidable sight

Following page: An adult Bonxie will stop at nothing to defend its nest so try and avoid straying into any territories.

regurgitate their catch, only for the Bonxie to gather it up. These high-speed chases can be focused on almost any seabird although they seem to have a preference for pursuing Gannets, often even catching hold of a wing-tip or tail-feather and forcing the bird into the water.

Bonxies will stop at nothing to obtain food and if not chasing down seabirds for a regurgitated meal they focus their attention on the bird itself. Most things that move either seem to represent a walking or flying meal, or a threat. On many islands species such as Puffins and even Rabbits become a fixed part of the diet, while any tired or sick bird will also be opportunistically consumed.

Bonxie colonies are intimidating places. The breed out on open coastal grassland and moorland with colonies consisting of anything from 1–2 pairs up to 1,000 pairs. They defend their nests with vigour and if you venture to any of the seabird-dominated islands of northern Scotland you are likely to experience first-hand the undiminishing ferocity with which they will see you out of their territory. Adults take flight at the approach of an intruder and gain height rapidly. An about turn and they start hurtling downwards aiming for the head of the potential threat whether that be a person, a dog, a sheep or some other interloper. At the last minute they pull up, often displacing careful styled quiffs, with the whoosh of wings. This attack is a heart-pounding experience and generally elicits a hasty retreat by the observer, although where skua densities are high the attacks can be relentless. The Bonxie is the only species in the UK that has directly caused a human fatality so the threat is a real one and many people have been clipped by sharp claws resulting in impressive blood wounds.

WHEN AND WHERE

Bonxies are summer migrants and arrive back on their breeding grounds in April and May, remaining until September and even October. They are generally colonial although isolated pairs do occur. You should avoid entering colonies both for the birds' welfare and for you own. There are however a number of sites where birds can be seen well without disturbing breeding. Shetland and Orkney are strongholds and sites such as Hermaness RSPB and Mousa RSPB off the south-east coast of Shetland are great places to see Bonxies at their best. On the mainland Duncansby and Dunnet Heads, Caithness, are the best places to observe Bonxies patrolling the cliffs in search of unsuspecting auks, while Handa Island in north-west Sutherland is also a superb place to watch these, and many other seabirds.

24. TUBENOSE COLONIES

Tubenoses are true seabirds. In the UK we have four breeding species – Fulmar, Manx Shearwater and European and Leach's Storm-petrels – with a number of other passage and vagrant species of albatross, shearwater, petrel and storm-petrel on the list. These are collectively called tubenoses due to the presence of a tubular structure along the top of the beak. This is used for expelling salt which is ingested during their lives at sea. Most of us will have seen Fulmars well, and possibly even shearwaters and storm-petrels at sea, but have you ever seen them at their breeding colonies? The Fulmar is easy to see on breeding cliffs due to its diurnal nature, and habit of breeding on ledges, and while common it makes them no less impressive as they master the updrafts and the eddies of air accentuating their skills on the wing. Their guttural cackles give the impression of ill-tempted old people, bemoaning their cliff-ledge neighbours, and the quarrels and jostling that frequently ensue are well worth watching.

For the remaining species, their activity around breeding colonies is restricted to the hours of darkness. After long foraging trips, often covering hundreds of miles out to the edge of the continental shelf, storm-petrels and shearwaters return to their burrows and rock-clefts. They are colonial, and colonies are often on a monumental scale. The island for Rum is impressive to look at; a domineering mountain erupts from the Hebridean Sea, rivalling neighbouring Skye in scenic terms. During the day the upland grasslands of this mountain remain relatively quiet, being patrolled by eagles and grazed by Red Deer, but by night 100,000 pairs of Manx Shearwaters can leave and return to their burrows. Unusually for the UK, much of the colony is located more than 600m (2,000ft) above sea-level. Having gathered in rafts offshore prior to dusk, they fly back in towards their burrows as night falls, filling the air with the sounds of wing-beats and the eerie wails they produce. Their final approach to the burrow normally involves a thud as they hit the ground, and a quick, ungainly scamper until out of sight and harm's way underground. Further south, off the coast of south-west Wales, 45,000 pairs breed on Skokholm and 120,000 pairs breed on nearby Skomer.

Storm-petrels are even more fascinating. They are incredibly abundant breeders yet still remarkably little is known about them due to their tendency to nest on remote rocky islets well away from human habitation. By night they enter the rocky crevices, burrows and gaps in dry stone walls in which they breed, and from here they sing. The song is less of the melodious and more of a purr interspersed with clicks – famously described as 'like a fairy being sick'! At the height of summer in northern Scotland darkness never fully arrives and the 'simmer dim' as it is known maintains enough of a glow to be able to see these bat-like birds as they whirr around their colonies, often in the tens of thousands. One of the greatest tubenose experiences of all is assimilating

Above: A Manx Shearwater returns to its burrow under the cover of darkness.

Following spread, left above: Fulmars return to their breeding sites and start displaying early in the year.

Following spread, left below: Skomer, Pembrokeshire, hosts hundreds of thousands of pairs of Manx Shearwaters. By day shearwater and petrel colonies appear deserted, and the birds are easy to overlook.

the sight, sound and smell of European Storm-petrels as they flit around the 2,000-year-old Broch of Mousa, off the east coast of Shetland.

To experience Leach's Storm-petrels at night you will have to venture out to the very limits of British territory, and the islands of St Kilda. Here the imposing Hirta offers shelter for both humans and birds alike and weather permitting you may be able to camp in the village. The island also harbours some of the other birding spectacles listed in this book (see also 23. Bonxies 20. Seabird Colonies, including hundreds of Puffins and thousands of Gannets) and the resident Soay Sheep.

Above: It's hard to believe that tiny, frail-looking European Storm-petrels spend most of their lives on the open oceans.

WHEN AND WHERE

Fulmars can be found on many cliff ledges around the UK coasts, however the most spectacular colonies are found in Scotland with islands such as Foula, Shetland, hosting thousands of pairs on stomach-churningly high cliffs, for instance the Kame, which is 1,233ft (376m) of sheer cliff! Just a few of the sites include: Sumburgh and Hermaness, both Shetland; Dunnet and Duncansby Heads, both Caithness; Handa Island, Sutherland; Isle of May, Fife; Flamborough Head and Bempton Cliffs, Yorkshire; and South Stack, Anglesey.

The nocturnal tubenoses are considerably harder to see and require a great deal of care to avoid damage and disturbance to the colonies. Accessible colonies are listed as follows. Manx Shearwaters can be watched on: Rum, Inner Hebrides; Skokholm, Pembrokeshire; and Bardsey Island, Gwynedd. European Storm-petrel colonies are at Mousa, Shetland, and Skokholm, while Leach's Storm-petrels are on St Kilda, Outer Hebrides. On Skokholm you can stay at the observatory where the wardens will show you incubating shearwaters, and even storm-petrel chicks (in August). Prior arrangement is normally required to visit all these colonies and guided tours can be joined to maximise your enjoyment of the spectacle and minimise any impacts. If visiting St Kilda you will need to arrange camping as well as drop-off and pick-up.

25. TURTLE DOVES

We have strong cultural connections to Turtle Doves. They are simultaneously an emblem of devotion, and a symbol of both hope and despair in the conservation world. The song is one of the most welcome sounds of spring and summer. The soft purring from which it gets its name – the anglicisation of the French word *tourterelle* – is actually onomatopoeic. The song was formerly typical of classic English landscapes such deciduous woodland edges, thick hedgerows and lush field margins; a sound that really signalled the start of summer. Nowadays many areas where it formally occurred are deprived of this purring song. The Turtle Dove population has suffered a 91 per cent decline since 1995 and the range has contracted considerably from what it used to be. Where flocks of 100 once foraged only single birds can now be found.

The sleek yet shy Turtle Dove is a beautiful bird to look at, with subtle hues of pink blue, grey and cream contrasting with an almost tortoiseshell-like pattern of brick-red and black scalloping on the folded wing. It has a bold four-striped neck-pattern and a striking black, white and grey tail-pattern, while the bright yellow iris is surrounded by vivid red skin. Everything about this bird shouts class and elegance.

Turtle Doves are highly migratory and our British breeding birds spend the winter in Africa, migrating south through France, Italy and Spain and across the Sahara. One of the biggest pressures they face comes from the hunting fraternity, for whom Turtle Dove shooting is a very popular pastime. A combination of hunting, disease and agriculture changes leading to food shortages are thought to be responsible for the huge crash in the population.

This beautiful and charismatic bird thoroughly deserves our support. You can find out more about the work that is being undertaken to help the species on the Operation Turtle Dove website which is raising both awareness and funds for this declining species. There are also schemes and suggestions on how best we as individuals can hope to improve the fortunes of Turtle Doves, including by attracting them into gardens.

If you go in search of Turtle Doves take the time to enjoy them, to appreciate

their stunning plumage and lazy summer song, and to take in the entire ambience of the place.

Above: Turtle Dove numbers have plummeted in Britain and the species needs all the help it can get.

WHEN AND WHERE

Turtle Doves normally return to the UK in late April and May, and depart in September. They were formally distributed across southern and eastern England, as far north as North Yorkshire, and as far west as eastern Wales. Nowadays this range is much contracted with Turtle Doves extinct in Wales, virtually absent from south-west England, and elsewhere found in densities throughout much lower than they were just a decade ago. Some sites have held on to their Turtle Doves and these include: Minsmere RSPB, Suffolk; Fowlmere, Cambridgeshire; Otmoor, Oxfordshire; and Frampton Marsh, Lincolnshire.

GET INVOLVED

Why not support the superb work of Operation Turtle Dove by reporting a sighting, or even creating some good Turtle Dove habitat. You can find out more at: www.operationturtledove.org

26. SWIFTS

Ah, Swifts! They are the quintessential sound of summer. They bring a smile to every birder's face and even to those with little knowledge of this phenomenal species. Swifts have become synonymous with all things connected with the British summer; a sound track to a cricket match on the village green, a parting acknowledgement of day as balmy dusk falls on a summer's evening, a herald of brewing thunderstorms, and a signal that summer has both finally arrived, and in turn ended.

Even without the cultural and seasonal connections Swifts are a marvel. A superbly honed flying machine that towers up into the blue only to descend at the end of the day to return to a nest site in a roof cavity. In the UK we are fortunate enough

to see many aspects of their behaviour from migration to breeding. When they first arrive, often as one of the last migrants back in May, they make their presence known with high-pitched screams, and low-level, break-neck flights along streets and over rooftops. Indeed it is this exact behaviour that is the difference between a dull day and an enlivened day for me as I work in the office.

Swifts are the champions of the air. They can remain on the wing for 10 months of the year, sometimes even longer, and recent research has shown that they spend 99 per cent of their time in flight once they've left their breeding grounds, often climbing to altitudes of

Above: Swifts are the masters of the air, capable of travelling huge distances in a single day and thousands of miles without landing.

Opposite: Swifts are some of the last summer migrants to appear in Britain each spring, and their arrival en masse generally signals the start of summer.

Following page: The sound of Swifts screaming through our streets is the most quintessential summer bird call.

well over 2 miles (3km) at dusk. It is not uncommon for them to cover 500 miles (800km) over the course of a day, and they are particularly adept at using the Earth's pressure systems to their advantage, often covering over 1,000 miles (1,600km) in a single foraging trip which can involve skirting around a low-pressure system to feed on the billions of insects that gather in the warm air behind it. This can lead to some monumental movements of Swifts over the UK, with the birds often seemingly heading in the 'wrong' direction. These movements can happen almost anywhere at any time during the summer in response to weather conditions but the most dramatic spectacles tend to occur along the east coast of England. The

most reliable place to witness this is Spurn Peninsula, Yorkshire, where between about 20 June–10 July many thousands of birds can be seen moving through.

Before humans arrived Swifts would have bred on cliffs and in caves, but the development of huge cities suddenly afforded a plethora of breeding opportunities. As we have continued to evolve so to has the design of our buildings and we are now slowly but steadily constructing more insulated dwellings, to the detriment of Swifts. Where once numerous roof cavities existed, breeding opportunities are now gone and many streets have fallen silent in summer.

WHEN AND WHERE

Swifts can be seen almost anywhere in the UK between May and the end of August, however they become increasingly scarce the further north and west you move. They particularly favour old towns and buildings which generally afford easier access into roof spaces for breeding. Of the more famous Swift colonies, the central spire of the Oxford University Museum of Natural History is a great place to watch the dynamic activities of up to 60 pairs of Swifts. In fact both Oxford and Belfast are 'Swift cities' – conurbations that have been awarded Heritage Lottery Funding (through the RSPB) to maintain and enhance their Swift populations.

Swift migration along the Spurn Peninsula, Yorkshire, can be a spectacular experience. The bulk of this movement is thought to comprise either non-breeding birds or foraging breeders from continental populations. Other locations along the east coast including East Anglia can also experience large movements. If you want to enjoy a crazy melee of feeding and drinking birds then heading down to a local lake or reservoir at dusk offers the best chance of seeing this.

GET INVOLVED

You can create your own Swift experience by installing Swift boxes on or in your house – more information can be found at www.swift-conservation.org. Not only does this enhance your enjoyment of such an amazing bird but it helps to bolster the declining UK population.

27. MANX SHEARWATER AGGREGATIONS

We have covered the breeding exploits of these remarkable seabirds (see 24. Tubenose Colonies), and while their nocturnal exploits are outstanding, they come into their own when they are flying low over the water. Manx Shearwaters have been known to live for up to 60 years, each year migrating from their breeding grounds in the North Atlantic through the warm waters of the tropics to the cool upwellings off the coasts of Brazil and Argentina. In terms of physiology they are far better equipped for a life navigating the ocean than one scuttling around their island burrows. A bird first ringed on Bardsey Island, Gwynedd, in 1957 (which at the time was considered to be at least 5 years old) was retrapped in 2003 and during the intervening period it was estimated to have flown at least 5 million miles (8 million km). Further examples of their unparalleled flying abilities came from early experiments which took Manx Shearwaters from their burrows and released them in far-flung locations, recording the date and time of both the release from the departure location and the arrival back at the burrow.

The most extreme of these involved a bird released at Boston Airport in Massachusetts, USA, which navigated its way back to its burrow over a distance of 3,000 miles (4,800km) in just 12.5 days. Nowadays with increased technological capabilities we have been able to track other species making much faster migrations but this still does not detract from the immense ability of these birds to navigate the oceans. Further research suggests that birds from burrows on Welsh islands actively forage for prey in the Bay of Biscay – a journey involving a round-trip of over 750 miles (1,200km).

Much closer to home though we have an even more remarkable spectacle. For it to occur conditions have to be perfect. In mid- to late July a spawning event of fish

This spread and following spread: The Manx Shearwater feeding frenzy off Borth is joined by other seabirds such as Gannets and various species of gulls.

appears to occur at the mouth of the Dyfi Estuary, Ceredigion. Here, off the beaches of Ynyslas and Borth, huge aggregations of Manx Shearwaters can amass, sometimes numbering up to 50,000 birds. These aren't just distant flocks of pinprick birds, but inshore frenzies of activity with shearwaters cruising through the breaking waves of the beach, diving for the bounty of fish present, occasionally even flying over the shoreline. The flocks can almost appear like a huge organism with birds lifting, flying upwind or upstream of the tide, then frantically feeding as they get washed along the coast only to lift once move and move back to the start of the feeding flock. It is not an annual event, and when it does occur it is often a short-lived phenomenon, but these uncertainties make the spectacle even more sensational, and even more of an enigma. To witness it is to witness one of the greatest shows in British ornithology. The feeding frenzies also attract other birds such as Gannets and various species of gulls and terns, and it is worth scanning through the throng of Manx Shearwaters for the rarer Balearic Shearwater.

Large aggregations of Manx Shearwaters can be seen offshore from breeding colonies close to dusk. Birds gather together after foraging trips waiting for darkness to fall so that they can return to their burrows safely. In such cases they generally just rest on the water and are not engaged in feeding activities.

WHEN AND WHERE

This spectacle is highly ephemeral and sporadic, which makes it even more of a privilege to witness. The Ceredigion beaches of Borth and Ynyslas are the best places to see it, although it may also occur at other river mouths in Cardigan Bay, so for example it could be worth checking out the Mawddach Estuary to the north.

Look out for rafting shearwaters off any of the breeding colonies featured in the Tubenose Colonies section (24.), especially Bardsey, Rum and Skokholm.

28. TYSTIES

The Black Guillemot, or Tystie, is frequently overlooked but is a superbly charismatic auk. It gets this rather endearing name from the Old Norse *peisti* – an onomatopoeic name describing the remarkable high-pitched whistles the birds produce. These calls sound nothing like those of other auks and can be easily missed by the untrained ear. In fact some of the calls produced are so high that they are beyond the limits of what humans can perceive. It is however rather difficult to actually overlook this species in the summer months, when its striking piebald plumage, with large white wing-panels on an otherwise black body, is offset by flashes of red. In summer and winter plumage one of the most eye-catching things about these birds is their blood red legs, which are often noticeable as they up-end and head towards the seabed in search of their favourite prey, Butterfish. They can frequently be observed battling to down these long, writhing mauve-brown fish, so it's well worth spending a bit of time watching birds on the water. If you are

lucky enough to get close to them as they are calling you may also see the vivid red gape. Come winter they take on an altogether different but by no means less attractive appearance. The striking black and white plumage is lost and replaced by a far more subtle black, grey and white mottling, still emboldened by flashes of red from the gape and feet.

Unlike other auks Tysties favour inshore and sheltered waters, rarely venturing far offshore. One of the easiest places to see them is in harbours, sometimes even in very busy ports, where they can be found fishing just off the jetties and harbour walls. In such situations they can be particularly confiding, with the harbour walls offering

Above: Black Guillemots have taken full advantage of the work of humans; in spring they can often be seen calling from crevices in harbour walls.

Opposite: The striking piebald plumage of Tysties of contrasted by scarlet feet.

Following spread: Harbour-side holes provide perfect breeding burrows for Tysties.

a unique perspective on the birds with often point-blank views from an elevated observation position. Harbours not only provide excellent waters for fishing but also excellent sites for breeding. Many have old drainage holes in the walls and these artificial burrows make perfect breeding locations. You may find yourself eyeball-to-beady-eyeball with a confused Tystie if you peer slowly over the side of a seawall, and in certain locations the adults will sit at the mouth of these holes calling away to a partner on the water. In more natural surroundings Tysties favour boulder beaches, the bases of cliffs and rocky islets where they breed in cavities in the rocks.

WHEN AND WHERE

Tysties are widely distributed around the northern and western coasts of Britain with the highest concentrations in the Northern Isles and Hebrides. They breed as far south as Anglesey, the Isle of Man, southern Scotland and also very sporadically in north-east Scotland. They tend to be sedentary although birds can occasionally be found further south during winter.

The best time and place to see Tysties is in summer in Scotland. Many an exciting birding trip to more far-flung islands has started with great views of confiding Tysties in the harbour, and they can frequently be exceptionally approachable. While they are great to watch at any time of year the months of May and June offer the peak period of enjoyment for the observer with the birds showing their most pristine plumage and greatest amount of vocal activity during this period. In Scotland the best places to see them include: the seawall at Greenock, Clyde; Oban Harbour, Argyll; and Lerwick Harbour, Shetland. Their most southerly outpost is Anglesey, where Holyhead Harbour and Penmon Point offer the best chances of catching up with this charismatic species.

29. SWALLOW ROOSTS

It is said that 'one Swallow does not make a summer', but does 10,000 Swallows make the end of summer?

Swallow roosts too easily pass unnoticed. They are a treat to be savoured, an experience to be absorbed. Simply finding them can be something of a challenge, and too often the birds have dispersed before you have time to get there to see them. It was once thought that Swallows wintered buried in the mud at the bottom of ponds. Nowadays we know much more about Swallows and their phenomenal ability to migrate from the southern tip of Africa to our houses, barns, yards and villages year after year. They are symbols of spring and perhaps the most universally recognised of all our summer migrants, finding their way in to myth and legend, song and story, poem and rhyme. As we increasingly urbanise our country we are finding more and more that Swallows are being pushed out into the countryside, away from the majority of the populace, and as a result they are becoming increasing less connected with our lives.

They are still here though and still as important as ever. Most of us enjoy the first sightings of the spring – a single bird

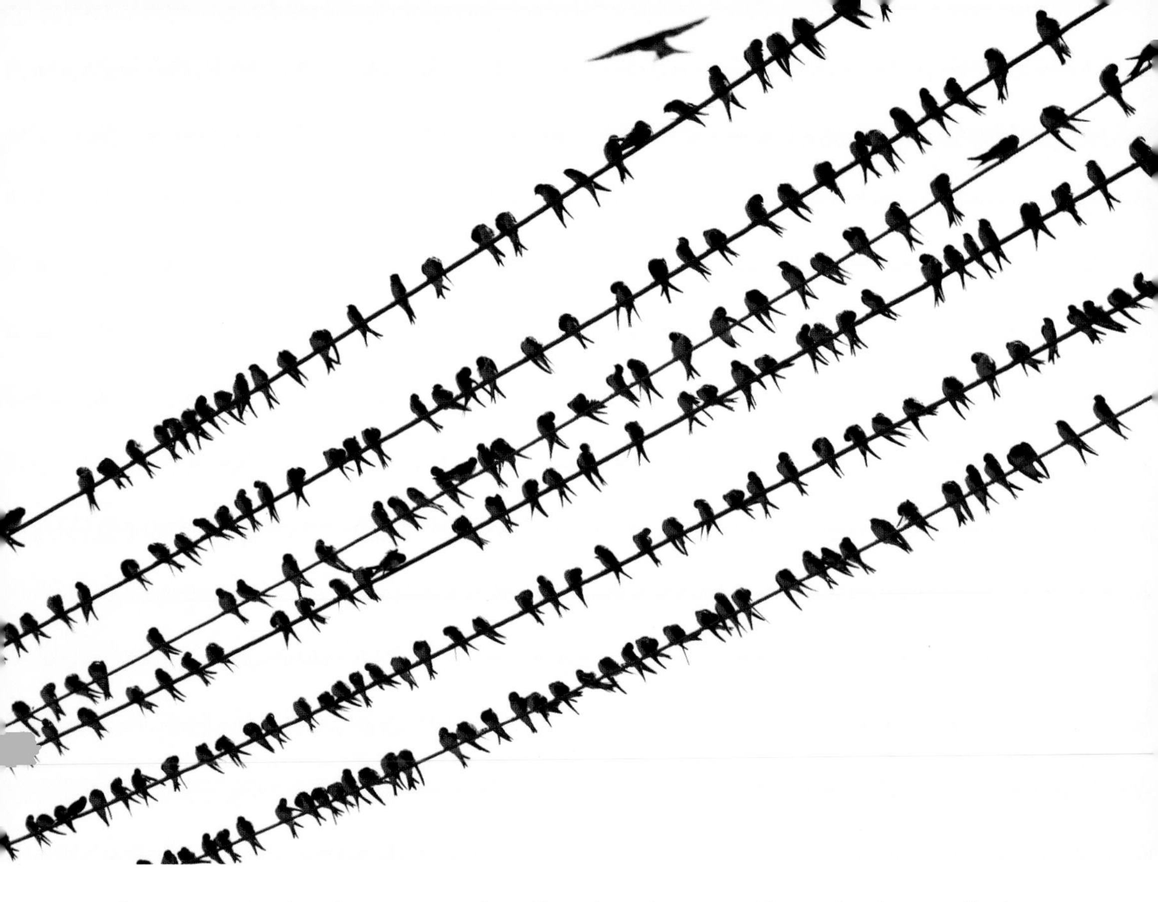

or small group winging its way north, often low into a northerly breeze, or towering high on those first warm spring days. As the population swells with new arrivals so breeding commences and by the end of the summer the population is at its maximum, supplemented by thousands of newly fledged juveniles and migrants from further afield. Villages start to see telegraph wires adorned in Swallows and House Martins, the air full of their delightful twittering, almost in excited anticipation of what lies ahead. As one they up and start their journeys south. For many this will be their first migration and it is a case of safety in numbers. As daylight starts to wane Swallows need somewhere safe to roost. Woodlands and scrub harbour too many predators so the favoured habitat is reedbeds. Flocks from all directions gather

Above: Swallows gathering on wires is a sure sign that summer is coming to an end.

Opposite: Hobbies and other raptors take advantage of gathering Swallows, often giving great views.

Following page: Roosting in large numbers provides protection from predators.

over favoured reedbeds, spiralling around in huge flocks. The diminutive size of the bird often escapes the observer's eye, even when thousands gather, however the continual chatter and chirrup of calls generally alerts you to their presence high above the reedbed.

Their descent into the reeds can be dramatic and rapid, often plummeting at break-neck speed from high up, levelling off just above ground height, skimming through the now browning flowering tops of the reeds and vanishing. Occasionally they will embark on test flights, and instead of dropping out of sight will spiral back up. This is when the likes of Hobbies and Sparrowhawks take advantage and the hunt is on. Flocks of Swallows form tight balls that tower into the sky alarm-calling as a hungry Hobby chases up behind them. Marshes are popular gathering spots for Hobbies during the day as they feed on dragonflies but many will remain and hunt for Swallows as dusk falls. Eventually the Swallows will plummet again towards the reeds and this time drop down onto their reed-stems. No sooner are they perched up in the reeds than the noise stops and you would be clueless to the presences of thousands of birds. No wonder it was thought that they spent the winter at the bottoms of ponds.

More recently the increase in maize crops has seen Swallows and House Martins roosting in crop fields. Just as in reedbeds the birds spiral high before plummeting into the crop and out of sight.

Finding roosts can be an enjoyable challenge. Swallow roosts will often persist for days and occasionally weeks but not all number tens of thousands. Towards dusk they can often be seen flying in tight groups directly towards the location of their roost. It is possible over a series of nights to follow these routes, plotting on a map the locations where you observe Swallows and the directions in which they are flying, before extrapolating the lines to reveal the location of the roost. Scanning a map in advance often helps to identify potentially suitable sites which can be checked.

WHEN AND WHERE

Swallow roosts are a late summer and early autumn spectacle with August and September the key months. The birds prefer reedbeds but will occasionally roost in crops. Favoured sites include: Stodmarsh NNR, Kent; Slapton Ley, Devon; Malltraeth Marsh RSPB, Anglesey; Kilconquhar, Fife, and Graemeshall Loch, Orkney.

AUTUMN

30. IN SEARCH OF RARITIES

Searching for rarities is one of the most exciting of all aspects of birding. Unlike twitching, birders will head out to a specific area to actively search for rare birds. The thrill is in the chase, the inevitable lows of not finding anything, and the ultimate elation at discovering a species thousands of miles from where it should be. Officially the term 'rarity' is used by the British Birds Rarity Commission (BBRC) to label those species that have turned up on fewer than 100 occasions over the past 10 years. In the context of the book though I will also extend it to include any species that for whatever reason is unusual in a particular location at a particular time.

Rarities are by definition unusual. They can hail from every possible point of the compass and in the past decade alone an exceptional number of new species has been added to the British List (which now numbers between 600–620 species, depending on the criteria used), including Glaucous-winged Gull, Long-billed Murrelet and Tufted Puffin from the Pacific, Eastern Crowned Warbler and Rufous-tailed Robin from the Far East, Allen's Gallinule from sub-Saharan Africa, Yellow-nosed Albatross from the South

Atlantic, and numerous North American and Asian landbirds. Many of these are vagrants, one-offs caught up in exceptional weather systems which deposit them in the UK. Others, such as those from the Pacific, are still vagrants but may be taking advantage of changing ice conditions in the High Arctic to move 'over the top' as such. The distribution status of many species is in continual flux. The first Ring-billed Gulls and Ring-necked Ducks (both species of North American origin) in the UK were recorded in 1973 and 1955 respectively, yet now both appear in small numbers annually. Today the once-rare Yellow-browed Warbler, which breeds in central Siberia, can be the commonest warbler species on certain days in autumn at some sites on the east coast. Conversely species such as Yellow-breasted and Rustic Buntings

Above: The Little Bunting is a regular but rare migrant in autumn most regularly found on northern islands and eastern headlands. Despite its regularity, it is still an exciting find.

Opposite: Careful scrutiny of common waders such as Dunlin may reveal transatlantic vagrants such as this juvenile Baird's Sandpiper, which made landfall in Cornwall.

Following page: British records of the North American Bonaparte's Gull have increased in recent years. This could be a result of more birds arriving, or improved ID skills among birders.

have become much more rare, largely as a result of the actions of humans, including deliberate exploitation.

We also see annual arrivals of scarce and rare birds from southern Europe. For example, Hoopoe, Bee-eater, Purple Heron and Glossy Ibis are all slowly becoming more frequent in the UK and occasionally even breeding, but would still constitute an exciting find for any one of us.

In general the majority of rare birds appear during the main migration periods of spring and autumn. Autumn especially can prove more predictable for those trying to find their own rarities. A series of strong westerly depression in late summer and early autumn is likely to deposit waders and possibly passerines from North America on our western coasts. A large high pressure system over eastern Europe draws winds from Siberia, over Scandinavia and down to the UK and frequently brings with it rarities between September and November. As a result rarity-hunters will try and put themselves in the best place possible to find anything

dropped in by these weather conditions and this often involves some of the most far-flung locations in the UK.

Trying to find rare birds is not for everyone. Many of the places that are best for rare birds can be bleak, windswept headlands or islands, and birds in general can be few and far between, especially if you are looking for North American birds which don't arrive with commoner migrants. It is entirely possible to spend 10 days searching every bush and ditch with no success, then out of nowhere something amazing might pop up in front of you. The excitement and elation of finding such a bird is difficult to describe. Most birders will say that they start shaking. There is often a frantic scramble to get a record shot (photo) of the bird and to get the news out to others before you can sit back and fully enjoy it. There are many other positives too; birding with friends and the teamwork that often goes into finding some of these birds is a great feeling, and enjoying watching something insanely rare is remarkably humbling.

WHEN AND WHERE

Rarities can turn literally anywhere and at any time, although there are most definitely peak times in occurrence and hot-spots that are worth checking. Coastal areas are nearly always the most productive but rarities can and do turn up in inland locations, although the difficulty is normally that most inland sites offer too much habitat in which birds can hide.

The best coastal rarity-finding locations are headlands and isolated areas of habitat, while estuaries and lagoons are well worth checking. If you are trying to find a particular species then try and and tap into its psyche and search its preferred habitats accordingly. True rarity hot-spots include: Foula and Fair Isle, Shetland; St Kilda, Outer Hebrides; Tiree, Inner Hebrides; Holy Island, Northumberland; Flamborough Head and Spurn Peninsula, Yorkshire; Blakeney Point and Wells Wood, Norfolk; Portland Bill, Dorset; the Isles of Scilly; and Bardsey Island, Gwynedd.

GET INVOLVED

If you find a rarity you should report it to the county recorder and also submit the record to the British Birds Rarities Committee (BBRC) for consideration. Why not challenge yourself and enter your local patch into the Patchwork Challenge (see www.patchworkchallenge.com) – finding a common species that's rarely seen in your area can be just as rewarding as finding a true national rarity.

31. SEAWATCHING

Spotting seabirds can be challenging, tantalising even, but also exceptionally rewarding. It provides a window into a world that is completely alien to us, and the opportunity to see species that are otherwise completely inaccessible in many cases (although some seabirds come to land in the UK on passage, to feed, or to breed, see: 14. Spring Skua Passage; 20. Seabird Colonies; 23. Bonxies; 24. Tubenose Colonies; and 27. Manx Shearwater Aggregations). Not only that, but these species are masters of their environment. Shearwaters and other tubenoses command the ocean winds and waves like nothing else.

You generally need two things for this experience – the sea and some rough weather. Luckily we live on an island that is frequently blasted by storms from all directions. Britain is also home to millions of seabirds and is positioned on the edge of the Atlantic Ocean, which all in all is a recipe for potentially good seawatching. For many, seawatching is an annual pilgrimage with birders descending on headlands in south-west England when the forecast looks promising. It can be particularly exciting on the lead-up to a trip watching an ever-deepening Atlantic depression swinging across the ocean on a collision course with the UK.

Birders gather in the half-light on favoured headlands, trying to hunker down in their prime spots from the previous day, week or even year, ready for a day of staring out to sea. A telescope is generally essential although you shouldn't neglect the immediate sea view as many a good bird has flown past a crowd of seawatchers undetected by the majority of birders, who have their scopes trained on the horizon.

One of the keys to the enjoyment of seawatching is making sure you are as comfortable as possible, and this includes being dressed in warm and waterproof clothing, having a hot flask and some food handy, and a decent chair or cushion. Position yourself correctly to maximise your view, minimise any salt spray or rain falling on your optics, and make sure you are able to hear if anyone else calls a good seabird flying by. Finally, expect to see nothing, as then anything that does pass by is a bonus! If seawatching with friends it is a good idea to establish reference points. You often hear people

calling a shearwater at 12 o'clock but never get on to it; one person's 12 o'clock is another person's 2 o'clock, and this is probably the biggest cause of confusion and irritation when seawatching, so be clear from the outset on where people are looking. The clock system is the most effective method and, combined with at-sea features (for example, buoys, islets and wind turbines), is generally the most reliable way of getting everyone on to a seabird dipping and banking through huge waves.

Once you are primed, comfy and equipped you could have one of the most exciting day's birding of your life. If nothing else you will probably witness hundreds of auks, Kittiwakes, and Gannets moving by. Depending on your location and the time of year seawatching can also result

Above: Grey Phalaropes are often displaced close inshore, and even move onto coastal lagoons during big autumn storms.

Following page: A Sabine's Gull is a fantastic find for any seawatcher. This is a juvenile.

in the observation of large numbers of seaduck and freshwater wildfowl, waders, and even passerines moving by, but most folk go in search of those hard-to-see pelagic species. With effortless motion large shearwaters – Great and Cory's – bank and glide over the waves and through the troughs. The former travel in a huge figure of eight route each year starting from their breeding grounds in the South Atlantic, and as they pass the UK they are starting their southbound journey. They can be abundant offshore, generally favouring the edge of the continental shelf, however when fast-moving weather systems swing in they can bring these ocean wanderers within sight of land. Sooty Shearwaters show more urgency to their flight and seem almost athletic as they power past. In contrast European Storm-petrels forage daintily with a bat-like flight over the surface, occasionally appearing to

freeze in mid-air before banking back to pick a morsel from the surface. Leach's Storm-petrels can get pushed inshore as well, particularly later in the season, while a true denizen of the Southern Ocean, the Wilson's Storm-petrel, can be found in with some regularity in very small numbers in south-western waters from June through until August.

Identifying seabirds can often be tricky, especially at great distance – some large shearwaters are often more than 3 miles (4.8km) away when you are watching them through a telescope – and it is always advisable to be cautious when claiming rare species, or seek the help of someone more experienced if necessary. If you are with other birders make every effort to get those around you on to any species of interest as all birders are keen on seeing these amazing ocean wanderers.

WHEN AND WHERE

The best locations are promontories or bays that funnel seabirds into them or past them. Peak times for seawatching are generally mid- to late summer into autumn, while winter wrecks can bring huge numbers of commoner seabirds close to shore at any time between November and February. During the summer months shearwaters, European Storm-petrels, skuas and terns tend to be the main quarry, while in autumn Leach's Storm-petrels, phalaropes, skuas and migrating wildfowl and waders are high on the list. Winter can produce vast numbers of Fulmars including 'Blue' Fulmars from further north, Leach's Storm-petrels and large numbers of auks and gulls.

Most sites have specific conditions which generate the best viewing and not every site produces the same species, for instance Cornwall has some of the best seawatching in the UK but you need to be at Porthgwarra in a south-westerly, and ideally one where the low hits the toe of Cornwall, to stand a good chance of large shearwaters, yet this site is not as good as Pendeen for smaller species such as Sabine's Gull, Grey Phalarope and Leach's Storm-petrel. Pendeen is generally best as the south-westerly winds swing north-west pushing seabirds close in. Sites like Pendeen are great for beginner seawatchers as views are closer and reference points more plentiful. Other prime locations include: Portland Bill, Dorset; Strumble Head, Pembrokeshire; Sheringham, Norfolk; Flamborough Head, Yorkshire; Frenchman's Rocks, Islay, Argyll; Machrihanish, Kintyre, Argyll; Butt of Lewis, Outer Hebrides; Dunnet Bay, Caithness; and North Ronaldsay, Orkney.

32. SCOTLAND'S EAGLES

Eagles are undoubtedly the most magnificent birds in our country. We are fortunate to have two species – Golden Eagle and White-tailed Eagle – both of which breed in Scotland. The former is one of Scotland's 'Big Five' and for good reason. Both species are monstrous and the White-tailed Eagle, with its 2.4m (8ft) wing-span, is frequently likened to a 'flying barn door'. The story of the White-tailed Eagle is one of success, but not without perseverance and continued effort from many individuals. The population of this species continues to grow thanks to many thousands of hours of protection, public engagement and work increasing awareness that have been invested in them. It is now very possible to drive along any section of road in western Scotland and hope to see a White-tailed Eagle. Unlike Golden Eagles they tend to be less concerned by human presence and more approachable, and are estimated to generate around £2 million a year for the local economy on Mull alone.

Eagles are far more than a means of income, though – they are the epitome of wilderness, a symbol of majesty, and a top predator clinging on where all other top predators have been eradicated. As a nation we should be immensely proud to have

these species as symbols of wilderness and conservation success. Unbelievably, eagles (as well as other birds of prey) are still occasionally targeted by some land managers and not a year goes by without an instance of poisoning or shooting. It is a very sad that in the 21st century we still have to fight to protect our most inspiring species from such selfish behaviour, which cannot be condoned in any way. If you ever witness any suspicious behaviour or find anything untoward in this respect, please make sure that you report it to the police to follow up.

Many people undertake an annual visit to Scotland with the sole intention of enjoying its unique diversity of birds and eagles are normally high on the list of 'must see' species. While there are a number of sites listed in this book that offer a strong chance of seeing eagles, finding your own is much more exciting. Eagles are protected by

Above: Any eagle encounter is one to remember and places such as Skye offer the chance to see multiple individuals of both White-tailed and Golden (pictured) together.

Opposite: Golden Eagle – majestic, awe-inspring and well worth the effort to see.

Following pages left: An immature Golden Eagle, aged by the extensive white tail-base and white base to the primaries.

Following page right: White-tailed Eagles can give superb views along the coast where they forage for discarded fish.

law and therefore birders should not go wandering over mountains and hillsides in search of them, especially during the breeding season. However there are plenty of places where eagles can be seen from public roads, and given their often huge territories this negates the need to go wandering into places where you could potentially cause disturbance to them.

White-tailed Eagles are predominantly coastal in Scotland and can frequently be found on sea loch islets and sheltered sections of coast, while Golden Eagles can be found in any rugged landscape from sea-level to the tops of Munros. In some areas, such as Skye, the density of eagles is exceptionally high and multiple individuals of both species can be observed circling together on occasions.

Witnessing a hunt is a very rare occurrence, however seeing Golden Eagles displaying is a far more frequent event if you know when and where to look. Territorial activity commences in early winter and lasts through until March. Adults can be seen rollercoastering over mountain ridges at breakneck speed. They often favour the highest ridgelines, and while views can be distant the sense of greatness is by no means diminished. An immature Golden Eagle wandering into an adult's territory can also provoke a similar response. White-tailed Eagles can also form small aggregations at times and it may be possible to see several birds in close proximity to each other.

Some of the best White-tailed Eagle encounters can be from boats with birds foraging and hunting along the coast and over water. There are two popular boat trips on Skye and one on Mull that offer birders great views of eagles from the sea.

WHEN AND WHERE

Golden and White-tailed Eagles are year-round residents of Scotland, although some dispersal by immatures and adults does occur during winter, as well as wider movements by immature birds in spring, especially White-tailed Eagles. Satellite-tracking has shown that both species can roam over much of Scotland as immatures, with one White-tailed Eagle from southern Ireland even crossing the whole of Ireland and Scotland and ending up on Orkney, before retracing its path and returning to its starting point. The best areas are without a doubt the west coast and the Highlands of Scotland. Key areas include: Loch Gruinart RSPB, Islay, Argyll; Colonsay, Argyll; boat-trips from Portree, including onboard the *Brigadoon* and *Stardust*, Skye; Gruinard Bay, Highland; Mull Eagle Watch and Sealife Surveys boat trips, Tobermory, Mull, Argyll; Harris, Outer Hebrides; Findhorn Valley, Highland; and Loch Leven, Perthshire (the last site hosting birds from a recently reintroduced population).

33. MIGRATING GEESE

There is nothing like the sound of migrating geese to signal the end of summer and the start of autumn. The honking, yipping, winking calls combined with the beautiful 'V'-formations as wave after wave passes south is one of the most uplifting experiences in nature. You often find that the first arrivals of geese correspond with a change in the weather, as a light northerly airflow can help the birds on their journey south but also brings with it cool, frosty, but clear mornings.

Britain sits in a pivotal location for many species, not least geese. Warmed by the Gulf Stream yet still comparatively far north, Britain provides just what geese breeding at higher latitudes require. They arrive from just about every northerly location possible – Brent Geese from Arctic Canada and Russia; Pink-footed Geese from Greenland, Iceland and Spitsbergen; Barnacle Geese from Greenland and Spitsbergen; White-fronted Geese from Greenland and Russia; and Greylags from Iceland – a combined total of some 825,000 geese descend on the UK to spend the winter. While species will overlap in their ranges it is generally more common to find large flocks of one species with the occasional lost cousin loitering within them. In fact its not uncommon to find a flock of a thousand geese with three

or even four other species represented within it.

While most people will be familiar with the large wintering concentrations of geese in places such as Norfolk, Lancashire, the Solway Firth, north-east Scotland, and Islay, this account focuses on experiencing the actual migration of these birds as they make their way to these wintering grounds – on the enjoyment of seeing birds move, the appreciation of exactly what they are capable of achieving, and the hurdles they have to endure to get to our shores.

For those Pink-footed Geese arriving from Greenland and Iceland, and to a lesser extend those species from the east, there are obvious and preferred routes that are followed by migrating flocks and if you get lucky with your timings you may find yourself in exactly the right place at the right time to witness a huge migration of

Above: Barnacle Geese pause while on migration.

Opposite: The sight of geese migrating south is a sure sign that autumn has arrived. These birds are Pink-footed Geese.

Following spread: Brent Geese migrating low over the sea.

geese. While many will take an almost direct line from staging sites in Iceland south towards the UK, some will filter down through the Northern Isles, and as they do so smaller flocks amalgamate into larger waves of birds, which then cross over the Pentland Firth to mainland Scotland. From here they often follow the edge of the Moray Firth before cutting across it into north-east Scotland. There is then a direct route south-west along the Aberdeenshire coast to Angus, where tens of thousands of birds gather to feed at the Montrose Basin. Some will linger in this area over winter while other will continue south with a last push through southern Scotland and onwards to Lancashire.

If you want to enjoy watching Barnacle Geese arriving then it is possible to see flocks arriving from Spitsbergen along the east coast of Britain. These will frequently then track north or south, depending on where they make landfall, before heading inland, bound for the Solway Firth. On the west side, try finding a prominent headland or a sea loch to watch along, ideally facing north or north-west. A north-westerly breeze pushes Barnacle and White-fronted Geese closer in towards, and over, the coast and it is possible to see hundreds migrating down the west side of Scotland on some days, often against impressive back-drops and with eagles on show to boot.

Brent Geese tend to track in low over the sea and the Norfolk and Suffolk coasts are probably the best places to see Brent Goose migration in action. Many thousands also winter along the south coast of England and headlands such as Selsey Bill, West Sussex, can be good for observing migration.

WHEN AND WHERE

The first Pink-footed Geese tend to arrive back in early to mid-September and the exact timing of mass arrivals often depends on the weather conditions but generally occurs in mid- to late September. Barnacle Geese tend to appear in early to mid-October and White-fronted Geese in mid-October, while Brent Geese generally arrive in late September. Key locations for witnessing goose migration are: Sheringham, Norfolk; Ardnave Point, Islay, Argyll; Trotternish, Skye; Noss Head, Caithness; Montrose Basin, Angus; and Loch of Strathbeg, Aberdeenshire.

WINTER

34. STARLING MURMURATIONS

A huge flock of Starlings moves as if it is a single organism, almost like a giant single-celled animal. As multiple flocks arrive in the same airspace it can be almost like watching an enormous lava lamp as these huge masses twist and stretch, condense and widen. Sometimes these swarms of birds coalesce, forming an inky black slick which pulses and contracts through the sky. Starling murmurations are simply breathtaking.

If you are really close to a flock you can sometimes hear the wing-beats of individual birds as they whirr overhead – they are almost stridulatory in tone. From a distance a sudden change in direction by a super flock can sound like waves breaking on a pebble beach. It seems impossible to our eyes that so many birds can all change direction at such high speed without ever colliding with each other. The sound these birds produce in flight gives rise to the collective noun, a murmuration.

During the day flocks of Starlings forage out across pastoral lands in search of grubs. They roam widely and can cover large distances over the course of

a single day. As the day draws to a close flocks start to think about roosting and begin converging on favoured spots to spend the night. Flocks pitch and wheel over their intended roost site and as numbers gather and activity intensifies it inevitably draws the attention of predators. Merlins, Peregrines, Hobbies (in summer), Sparrowhawks and Goshawks can all be drawn in to these whirling balls of 'fast' food, often with spectacular results. Flocks morph as raptors tear through them trying to snatch a straggler. Often this mass of birds will encircle a bird of prey while still keeping their distance as it endeavours to approach closer. Of course with such vast flocks a few casualties are inevitable and a daytime inspection surrounding these roosts can frequently

Preceding spread: Waxwings will brighten up any winter's day.

Above: A murmuration of Starlings at Shapwick, Somerset. Following the performance the flocks drop into the reedbed to roost.

Opposite: Starling murmurations form dynamic inky-black shapes in the dusk sky.

Following page: Starling murmuration over a pier.

reveal a peppering of plucked wings, feathers, feet, and bills.

As the light finally fails they stream out of the air and on to their perches with chattering, jangling, wheezing excitement. When roosting in reedbeds they skim low over the tops causing the reeds to quiver with the air movement. Discerning any one bird is impossible as they simple form a giant black entity pouring through the reeds. Unlike with Swallows (see 29. Swallow Roosts) the noise does not stifle after all the birds are down, instead the excited chatter continues, slowly dying away until the sky is black and the air silent.

WHEN AND WHERE

Starling murmurations are mainly a winter phenomenon with birds from the UK supplemented by waves of continental immigrants. Many of these birds have travelled thousands of kilometres to come and feed in the pastures of Britain. They are found throughout the UK and roosts can occur anywhere from sea-cliffs to cities and woodlands to reedbeds. Some of the best displays are over coastal and marshy areas where uninterrupted skylines offer the best views of the amazing aerial acrobatics.

Murmurations are best observed during the hour leading up to darkness as birds gather at roost sites from the wider countryside. Find a prominent place to stand and watch, then wait and enjoy. Traditional and accessible locations include:

Malltraeth Marsh RSPB, Anglesey; Otmoor RSPB, Oxfordshire; Ham Wall, Somerset; Newport Wetlands, Gwent, Gretna Green, Dumfries and Galloway; Brighton Pier, East Sussex; and Aberystwyth Pier, Ceredigion.

GET INVOLVED

Many reserves hold special dusk and dawn events enabling people to enjoy the arrival of Starling flocks and their settling in to roost. See reserve websites for more details.

35. RAPTOR AND CRANE ROOSTS

Dusk is often a brilliant time to track down otherwise mobile and difficult-to-see species. It is made even easier if the species in question have regular roost sites, and better still if these roost sites are communal. Luckily some birds of prey have just that. All raptors are exciting but seeing them hunting low over marshes as they arrive at roost sites is often one of the most enjoyable birding experiences. The end of the day signals one final opportunity to feed and many species will hunt right up to the point they arrive at their roost. Raptor roosts are generally associated with boggy ground, whether small areas of willow carr within marshes, or slightly drier clumps of rush that offer cover, are dry enough, and are sufficiently remote to inhibit attacks by ground predators at night.

Our dusk roost vigils often focus on just a few key species and these include Hen and Marsh Harriers, Merlin and Peregrine, and also Barn and Short-eared Owls. Given the wetland habitat preference of many raptor roost sites it can also be possible to see egrets and herons, including Bittern, making dusk flights to and from these areas, and even more excitingly Cranes.

Cranes were driven to extinction in the UK nearly 400 years ago, but a tiny nucleus

of birds recolonised the Norfolk Broads towards the end of the 20th century with a pair arriving in 1979 and breeding successfully in 1981. Since then numbers have built slowly but steadily. More recently the support of the Great Crane Project has bolstered the population further and following reintroductions birds are now seen with regularity on the Somerset Levels and up the Severn Estuary. Meanwhile the original recolonising nucleus has slowly spread across East Anglia and into the Fens, as well as pushing north onto other large, undisturbed bogs.

The mix of raptors and waterbirds at these roosts is hard to beat. Add in a sense of anticipation and some atmospheric meteorological conditions and it makes for a truly special evening.

Above: Any evening involving a Short-eared Owl is a good evening!

Opposite: The marshes of the Norfolk Broads, especially those at Hickling Broad's Stubb Mill, are particularly good for roosting raptors and Cranes.

Following spread, above: A good roost of Marsh Harriers can contain dozens of birds.

Following spread, below: The increasing number of Cranes in Britain signifies a welcome revival of a once-lost breeding species and is testament to dedicated conservation efforts.

Activity can often be driven by the weather and cold days frequently see more action from the birds. A light breeze can favour heightened activity from species such as harriers as it aids hunting. Harriers often quarter in over the marsh, occasionally tussling with one another. Merlins and Peregrines frequently make a hurtling pass before finding a perch, and the owls patrol silently and slowly. These places are never silent either. Ducks and geese generally add a constant murmur, Snipe start becoming active, rocketing into the air with a sharp calls as dusk approaches, while the squeals of Water Rails cuts through the air.

At places such as Stubb Mill, which is located beside Hickling Broad in Norfolk, the Cranes announce their arrival with the most heart-palpitating of calls; a deep and resounding, almost trumpeting *krroo* or *gruuu*. Hearing this sound in the UK always runs a shiver of excitement down my spine. The excitement is intensified as the Cranes slowly flap in over the misty marshes above dozens of harriers. Indeed the Stubb Mill roost of Marsh Harriers can number over 100 birds, not to mention all the other raptors present. Each site is different and the roost at Parkgate Marsh, Cheshire, can be particularly action-packed if dusk coincides with a high tide. On spring tides the whole marsh disappears under the sea but slightly more moderate tides serve to push birds closer to the viewers as they endeavour to retreat from the advancing sea and keep hunting.

WHEN AND WHERE

Raptor and Crane roosts are most active and best viewed during the winter months. Many smaller roosts are scattered all over the country and most are difficult if not impossible to view safely or without disturbing the birds. The best and most accessible sites are: Stubb Mill, Hickling NWT, Norfolk; Stodmarsh RSPB, Kent; Arne RSPB, Dorset; Llanrhidian, Camarthenshire; Parkgate Marsh, Cheshire; Blacktoft Sands RSPB, Yorkshire; Westhay Moor SWT, Somerset; Great Fen CWT, Cambridgeshire; and Slimbridge WWT, Gloucestershire.

GET INVOLVED

Why not volunteer to take part in the Hen Harrier winter roost survey, which is organised through the Hawk and Owl Trust? You can find out more at: http://hawkandowl.org/our-work/research/hen-harrier-winter-roost-survey/

You can also find out more about Crane sightings on the Great Crane Project site at: www.thegreatcraneproject.org.uk/seeing-cranes/sightings-map

36. RED KITE FEEDING STATIONS

Driven to the very brink of extinction in Britain, the Red Kite clung on only in the remote and undisturbed oak woodlands of Mid Wales, where thankfully its fortunes finally changed. Through decades of protection from egg collectors the population slowly started to increase in Wales, all thanks to the immense dedication of individuals and nature conservation organisations. From 1989 a reintroduction scheme was launched in Scotland and England which proved very successful. Nowadays there are in excess of 1,600 pairs of Red Kites breeding in Britain and they have become so numerous in some areas that they can even be considered a garden bird in some parts of the Home Counties.

The Red Kite is particularly gregarious for a raptor and these birds can frequently be found breeding, feeding and roosting close to each other. Whilst they will take live prey they are particularly adept at scavenging and spend much of the spring and summer 'cleaning' the hillsides of afterbirth and other bits of carrion. This penchant for bits of meat has led to the appearance of a number of Red Kite feeding stations where food is placed out once a day for the kites to scavenge. This act of feeding Kites has on occasion been criticised, however it is no different to feeding any other bird and the opportunity it presents to engage people with wildlife should not be underestimated.

The most spectacular of the feeding stations is in the core range of the Welsh Red Kite population, just outside Rhayader. Here, at Gigrin Farm, up to 600 Red Kites can gather to feed, wheeling around above the fields and swooping in low and fast to snatch a tasty morsel. The whinnying calls of the Kites which adds to the experience. Most of the year there are fewer birds than this present but it is no less of an extravaganza and it can even make for better viewing when a single bird can actually be followed for a prolonged period. As well as the kites, Buzzards, Ravens and Carrion Crows also gather to feed. Many of the feeding stations also have dedicated photography hides which allow an even closer encounter with these stunning birds.

Feeding stations in Scotland don't attract as many birds simply because the population isn't as large, but they are still well worth a visit. Bellymack Hill Farm in Dumfries and Galloway is on the Galloway Kite Trail and can attract up to 100 kites.

WHEN AND WHERE

There are now a number of feeding stations around the UK with two in Wales – Gigrin Farm, Rhyader, Powys; and Red Kites Wales feeding station, Llanddeusant, Carmarthenshire – and three in Scotland – Bellymack Hill Farm, Laurieston, Dumfries and Galloway; Argaty, Doune, Perthshire; and Tollie, Dingwall, Highland. In the Home Counties there is a reliable roost site for Red Kites at Whitehall Wood, Hertfordshire, where up to 100 birds can be seen.

Peak numbers occur during the winter months but most feeding stations will have activity through the summer as well.

Left: A Red Kite glides in to scavenge meat from a feeding station.

Opposite: Gigrin Farm, Powys, has been a top kite-watching spot for decades.

37. RING-NECKED PARAKEETS

In the introduction to this book I stressed the diversity of bird species present in Britain, and our long history of enjoying birds has led to many species being accidentally or deliberately introduced. The British List now contains many species that have had a helping hand arriving here, including Pheasant, Red-legged Partridge, and Little Owl, with more seemingly set to become established, such as Black Swan, Bar-headed Goose and a variety of parakeets. One of the most successful has undoubtedly been the Ring-necked Parakeet. First confirmed breeding in 1971, there are now an estimated 30,000 birds in Britain with the vast majority centred around London.

Their urban preferences, raucous calls and striking plumage make them a charismatic bird that attracts a lot of attention. Members of the public often enjoy seeing these birds while strolling around the London parks and they certainly add a splash of colour to a cold grey winter's day. There is however the possibility that the resounding success of this species could be detrimental to that of others and there is evidence from Belgium that Nuthatch abundance declined where parakeets proliferated.

Whether you consider them friend or foe they are for the time being firmly established on the British List and are a great attraction during a day exploring the capital. They favour mature parkland trees where they breed in tree cavities and feed on leaves, buds and fruit, although they have now learnt the benefits of garden bird feeders too. In Hyde Park and Kensington Gardens you can now feed the parakeets by hand, while in Kew Gardens they make a superb aside to the stunning specimen trees.

One of the most exciting city birding experiences is watching Ring-necked Parakeets flying in to roost. Their elegant profile and rapid flight is exaggerated as groups of birds race over roofs and trees towards the roost site, gathering numbers as they go until hundreds, if not thousands are present. The cacophony of noise alone is a spectacle. Roost sites can be short-lived and in some cases people have made every effort to discourage parakeets, with the result being that some of the sites listed below may no longer be active, so it is worth trying to get up-to-date information before visiting the sites.

The most impressive roosts to date have been up to 8,000 birds at Esher Rugby Club (although this roost is no longer active) and up to 5,000 at Wormwood Scrubs. Roosts can be mobile but are fun to try and track down. Birds tend to stream over at set times shortly before sunset and also follow straight routes directly to roost sites, which can allow you to triangulate the roost location.

Opposite: Britain's population of Ring-necked Parakeets has boomed in recent years.

WHEN AND WHERE

Ring-necked Parakeets are now abundant in and around London. They can be seen almost anywhere although the best locations are the larger parks and gardens, including Hyde Park and Kensington Gardens, Richmond Park and Kew Gardens. The largest roosts occur during the non-breeding season between October and March. Wormwood Scrubs Park is situated in west London just north of the A40 (Westway). Take Wood Lane north to Scrubs Lane. Alternatively you can catch the underground to East Acton and then walk 320m north-east along Erconwald Street to Wormwood Scrubs Park. Another good roost site is Sutcliffe Park, which is 1km north of the South Circular Road along the A20 – there can be several hundred parakeets roosting here.

38. WAXWINGS

The Waxwing is one of the most eccentric of all birds occurring regularly in Britain. It has everything going for it – a punk crest, bold colours, an instantly recognisable call, gluttonous behaviour, and the tendency to arrive en masse and often in streets and gardens right in the middle of our towns and cities.

Waxwings breed in northern Scandinavia and across the boreal forest of Russia. They are eruptive migrants, that is, we can have years when hardly any Waxwings appear at all, but in other years, when the berry crops fail in their normal wintering range, they push further south and arrive in Britain. Sometimes the arrivals are minuscule, occasionally just odd autumn migrants on headlands, other years it's just a few small flocks in favoured localities, but in good years we can see a deluge.

The full name is Bohemian Waxwing, correct in that it certainly an alternative, almost arty, and free-spirited bird, not so correct in that it does not originate from Bohemia (which is in the present-day Czech Republic). Its scientific name, *Bombycilla*, alludes to its eccentric plumage, and means silky tail. Waxwings are stunning to look at and can also be very confiding, allowing close-up views and frequently drawing

the attention of the public as they swarm over berry trees stripping them bare in days, sometimes even hours. They seem to always look annoyed, with crest slicked back or raised, black beady-eye glaring out from a dark face and dark bib. Their bills seem to merge straight into their heads, with an almost waxy appearance to them. The plumage is subtle tones of pastels: wheat, light salmon and burly wood. The wings have flashes of white, and each of the secondaries is tipped with a brilliant crimson teardrop. This is actually the flattened tip of the feather-shaft rather the feather-webs themselves. Each of the primary tips is fringed with a yellow or white arrow-mark. The under-tail-coverts are brick-red, and the tail like a paint brush, charcoal grey-black and dipped in sulphur-yellow at the tip. These combine to create a beautiful combination of subtle

Above: Urban Waxwings inspire interest in birds and their arrival is often seen as the hallmark of a cold winter to come.

Opposite: A good crop of winter berries could draw in a flock of passing Waxwings.

Following spread: A Waxwing gorges itself on winter berries.

and contrasting colours and plumage.

In some favoured locations numbers can be impressive and flocks of in excess of 1,000 Waxwings have been recorded. These flocks roam around in search of berry-bearing trees and descend like a plague, often stripping the trees bare in a matter of hours. Some studies have found that Waxwings consume berries at a rate of up to 1,000 berries per bird per day, which is several times their own body weight.

Watching this pillaging is quite something. Whirs of wings, berries going everywhere, Waxwings hanging, hovering, teetering and squabbling. It's a frenzy of activity. Flocks will frequently lift off the berry trees as if they are a single unit and swirl around coming to alight on roof tops, aerials and adjacent tall trees. In fact, the way that Waxwings line up on aerials and chimneypots is yet another of their endearing qualities. As mentioned in Garden Birds (see 1.), Waxwings frequently visit gardens and to enjoy this rumpus from the comfort of your home has got to be one of the best birding experiences there is.

WHEN AND WHERE

Large arrivals can occur at any time between November and February, although they tend to be most frequent in the earlier part of the winter. With birds arriving from Scandinavia it is unsurprising that the bulk of Waxwing sightings occur in the northern and eastern parts of the UK. Flocks can be remarkably consistent in the choices of the locations in which they appear, even if there is sometimes a gap of several years between visits. The best towns and cities for Waxwings include Aberdeen, Inverness, Aviemore, Glasgow, Newcastle, York, Sheffield and Norwich (no further information is given on these sites in the Gazetteer). You can find out more about Waxwing arrivals from the bird news services, as well as on Twitter and Facebook.

GET INVOLVED

If you are lucky enough to see Waxwings please report them for others to enjoy. You can tweet @WaxwingsUK or alert the news services such as BirdGuides and Rare Bird Alert via text, call, email or twitter. If you are watching Waxwings be sure to pay careful attention to their legs as recent winters have seen colour-ringing projects in northern and eastern Scotland which have helped to track the birds' movements during the course of each winter.

39. WINTER WADER FLOCKS

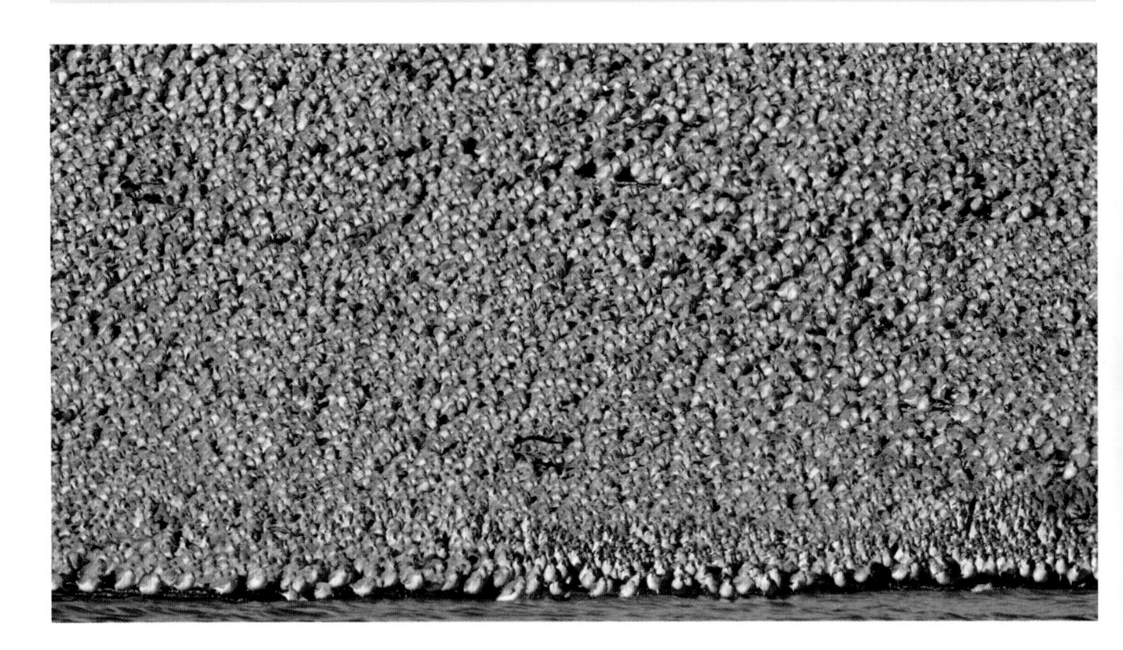

Every year British mudflats become home to thousands, if not millions, of waders during the winter months. Like so many other birds, waders migrate south along the East Atlantic Flyway from Arctic breeding grounds to feed in comparatively milder climates on intertidal areas that are rich in food. Some birds will spend the winter with us while others will continue south to Africa.

We are very fortunate to have many locations where we can witness the immense numbers and diversity of species that migrate to our shores. The biggest and best sites are estuary areas such as The Wash and the Humber in eastern England, which support approximately 350,000 and 150,000 waterbirds respectively, while the north-west estuaries and mudflats of Morecambe Bay and the Ribble also host 240,000 and 200,000 birds respectively. These are impressive numbers and there are many more coastal swathes supporting 50,000–150,000 birds.

The behaviour of these birds is driven by the tides. As the tide drops birds rush to make the most of the freshly exposed wet sand and mud, often following the edge

of the water. Feeding often appears to be frantic, like hundreds of clockwork toys milling around. The race is on as they only have a few hours before the tide turns and they start getting forced back up the shore. Watching the feeding behaviour of different species is fascinating and they are all adapted to prey upon certain invertebrates, with their bills equipped to either yank them out of the mud or prise apart shells. Curlew, Oystercatcher, godwits, redshanks, Dunlin and Ringed Plover are all segregated by how far their bills will reach into the mud and the type of prey they are after.

As the tide turns the waders are pushed back up the shore until no mud is left, and it is then that they are

Above: A flock containing Dunlin, Sandering and Ringed Plover takes flight.

Opposite: Wader flocks can be monstrous.

Following spread: Knot and Oystercatchers gather at the famous roost at Snettisham, Norfolk.

forced to seek an undisturbed area in which to see out the period of high tide. This is when the wader spectacles are at their best. The rising tide bunches birds together on ever-shrinking areas of mud. Occasionally the water outpaces the birds up the shore and forces hundreds, if not thousands, of birds into the air, whic then quickly descend again further up the beach. Eventually, with no shore left they billow, swish and swirl over the sea trying to find a roost site. Huge flocks glint in the sun as they bank and change direction. Golden Plovers can look especially golden on crisp winter days. Bands of silver and grey twist and writhe over the coast in an almost pained manner. Much like Starlings over a reedbed, many of the flights often seem choreographed and effortless, and also like Starlings they frequently attract unwanted attention so keep your eyes peeled for marauding raptors.

There are many places you can witness huge wader flocks during winter but most of the best spectacles are associated with spring tides. These exceptionally high tides occur monthly (check a local tide table), and force the birds even higher up the coast, occasionally removing all suitable roost options.

WHEN AND WHERE

Wader numbers start to build up in the autumn, and from November until March the mudflats are teeming with tens of thousands of birds. The Wash, and in particular Snettisham RSPB reserve, are home to the most renowned wader spectacles in the UK if not Europe, and waves of birds from the mudflats are forced up and over the seawall on spring tides, almost like a tsunami of birds at head height. Here they settle on the lagoons where they roost until the mud is exposed again. Watching both the flood and exodus of birds plus the ram-jammed banks of the lagoon is simply spectacular. Other brilliant places to witness huge wader flocks include: the Exe Estuary, Devon; Morecambe Bay, Lancashire; Point of Ayr, Flintshire, and Hoylake, Merseyside (both on the Dee Estuary); and Gibraltar Point, Lincolnshire.

GET INVOLVED

If you enjoy watching and counting waders then why not get involved with the BTO's Wetland Bird Survey (WeBS). This involves monthly counts of wetland birds along a predefined section of coast or water body. You can find out more at: www.bto.org/volunteer-surveys/webs

40. RAVEN ROOSTS

The Raven is one of our most intelligent and intellectually complex species. It is also one of the most successful species on the planet having colonised every habitat from the Arctic to the Sahara, from the bottom of the Dead Sea 1,400ft (430m) below sea-level to over 20,000ft (6,100m) up in the Himalayas, and from inner cities to the most remote wildernesses imaginable. They are opportunists, generalists and sometimes specialists capable of taking advantage of temporary food gluts, and also learning to forage, and even hunt, for specific species.

Culturally Ravens have deep roots connected with both life and death across North America and northern Eurasia. Our Nordic cousins revered Huginn and Muninn, two Ravens who bought news of the world to the god Odin. In more recent years they have been perceived as vermin in Britain, often with a bounty on their heads, and to this day many livestock farmers would still rather see them gone. Thankfully the law is now on the birds' side and following a population decrease to a low in the 1970s the population is now increasing.

They are also exceptionally social. Pairs bond for life and every day they engage

in a vast array of subtle displays, calling and frequent allopreening (when birds preen each other). Before they reach adulthood many younger birds form cohorts which often roam around the countryside in search of food, challenging territorial pairs and generally behaving mischievously to our eyes. These groups can often mass together at large food sources such as rubbish dumps and whale carcasses and there have been reports in the more distant past of up to 800 birds together at a carcass in Shetland. These days most birds are associated with areas of sheep farming and this is where the largest concentrations of Ravens can typically be found.

Anglesey may seem an unlikely location but it has held the second largest roost of Ravens in the world, peaking at just over 2,000 birds in the late 1990s and even today there are still several hundred birds present most nights throughout the winter. The roost is situated in Newborough Forest, a large conifer plantation abutting

Above and opposite: Social and intelligent, Ravens are fascinating to watch.

Following page: The distinctive deep *cronk* call of a Raven often indicates its presence long before the bird is seen.

long sandy beaches and the rocky island of Llanddwyn, and criss-crossed by a network of tracks. This site is the stage for one of the most eye-opening corvid spectacles in the world. Even on 'quieter' nights when only a few hundred birds come in, you can watch a catalogue of behaviours and listen to an entire language of communication. The Ravens tend to gather in open areas, on the beach and in forest clearings, and if there's a good westerly breeze the sand dunes provide the perfect updraft on which the birds can play, tumbling, flipping and gliding. During periods when the roost was most fully occupied, birds must have been travelling from a large area of Wales, and potentially even the Lake District, southern Scotland and Ireland (although not on a daily basis).

The sounds produced are sometimes incomprehensible, especially for a bird we so often associate with resonating *cronk* calls. Ticks, pops, whistles, cronks, croaks, and not to mention mimicry, sometimes of human-manufactured sounds; the language is rich in these roosts. They serve as important communication centres for Ravens and it has been shown that birds roosting alongside each other 'learn' where new food sources are.

Whether you visit the Newborough roost or try and find your own they are fascinating places full of remarkable behaviour. Some roosts are also shared. I remember once discovering a mixed roost of Golden and White-tailed Eagles and Ravens in a conifer plantation on Skye. Add in these two top predators and the behaviour element of pre-roost Ravens becomes even more fascinating. Not to mention the mind-boggling sight of eagles twisting and turning out of the marauding eagles way.

WHEN AND WHERE

Raven roosts can be occupied year-round although some are also ephemeral, linked with temporary food supplies. The largest numbers are normally found during the winter months, especially in January.

Ravens are found in highest numbers in western England, Wales, the Lake District and Scotland. The best bet for locating Raven roosts is to track birds as they fly in at the end of the day. The roost at Newborough Forest, Anglesey, is still active and attracts in birds from the entire island plus the mainland. Other roosts have been noted in the past from areas such as Aberfeldy, Perthshire, Skye, Shetland and Caithness. All these roosts were located in conifer plantations.

GAZETTEER

The following represents a full list of all sites referred to in the accounts. Acronyms are: NNR (National Nature Reserve), NP (National Park), NT (National Trust), NTS (National Trust for Scotland), RSPB (Royal Society for the Protection of Birds), WT (Wildlife Trusts).
Each site account includes:

■ Site, county – experiences at the site, cross-referenced to main text

■ Directions and notes on visiting and making the most of the experience.

■ Facilities and Accessibility: Cost, car parking, toilets, disabled access, other facilities.

■ Where relevant a web address link is also provided.

■ Many reserves offer free entry but rely on donations so please consider giving something if you have enjoyed your visit. Alternatively you can always join any one or more of the organisations that manage these sites.

Aberystwyth Pier, Ceredigion – *34. Starling Murmurations*

The seaside town of Aberystwyth lies on the edge of Cardigan Bay. The Starling roost occurs under the Royal Pier. It is best to arrive about an hour before dusk to enjoy the spectacular murmurations from the promenade.

■ Free ■ Car parking ■ Disabled access ■ All facilities in Aberystwyth www.aberystwythguide.org.uk/aberystwyth_starlings.shtml

---

Aber Valley NNR, Gwynedd – *16. Oak Woodlands*

A beautiful example of Welsh oak woodland 1.5 miles (2.4km) south of the A55 between Bangor and Llanfairfechan, acessed through the village of Abergwyngregyn. From the car park by the river the walk winds through woodland, pasture and coppice to the waterfall.

■ Free ■ Car park ■ Toilets ■ Disabled access (gradual incline to falls over gravel track) ■ https://naturalresources.wales/out-and-about/places-to-go/north-west-wales/coedydd-aber-national-nature-reserve/?lang=en

---

Aird an Runair, North Uist, Outer Hebrides – *14. Skua Passage*

The most north-westerly point of North Uist, 10 miles (16km) north-west of Carinish and close to Balranald RSPB reserve. Skuas prefer a north-westerly wind pushing them close in over the coast where they cut overland across the north end of North Uist and into the Minch. Mid- to late May sees the peak migration of skuas.

▪ Free ▪ Car park ▪ Toilets (Balranald)
▪ Access and facilities see below
▪ www.rspb.org.uk/reserves-and-events/find-a-reserve/reserves-a-z/reserves-by-name/b/balranald/about.aspx

Applecross mountain.

Applecross mountain, Sutherland – *11. Grouse (Ptarmigan)*

Applecross Pass (Bealach na Ba) offers one of the most accessible opportunities to see Ptarmigan. The minor road winds its way from the A896 (often hair-raisingly) up the mountain to the pass 6.8 miles (11km) north-west of Lochcarron – 0.4 miles (0.67km) beyond the crest of the pass is a right turn up to the radar station. Park here and walk up the road looking for Ptarmigan in the rocks on either side.

▪ Free ▪ Parking ▪ No facilities
▪ www.applecross.uk.com/msg/

Ardnave Point, Islay, Argyll – *33. Migrating Geese*

Parking for Ardnave is 3.5 miles (5.5km) north of Loch Gruinart RSPB, and is next to Ardnave Loch. From here walk out over the dunes to the head of the peninsula. Watch for geese (and swans) migrating in from the north down the sea loch. A great place for Chough, Twite, duck on the loch, and potentially even rarities.

▪ Free ▪ Car park ▪ No facilities
▪ www.islayinfo.com/islay-walk-ard-nave-point.html

Argaty Kite Feeding Station, Doune, Perthshire – *36. Red Kite*

Up to 30 birds visit the feeding station and visitors should arrive in time for feeding sessions (see website). Hides provide a comfy and concealed viewing platform.

▪ £6 adults, £3 children ▪ Car park ▪ Disabled access ▪ http://argatyredkites.co.uk/

Arne RSPB, Dorset – *21. Nightjar, 35. Raptor Roost*

Arne is a classic coastal heathland reserve supporting many rare and interesting species (and not just birds). There are many organised events which will introduce you to winter raptors and displaying Nightjars (see website for more details). Arne is situated on the south-west side of Poole Harbour.

From the A351 at the Stoborough Green roundabout take the northern exit into the village along Corfe Road. Continue for 0.2 miles (0.36km), taking the right turn along New Road up to Arne Road after 0.4 miles (0.7km). The reserve entrance is 2.8 miles (4.5km) along Arne Road.

■ Car park £2.50 per car for up to 2 hours (Free for RSPB members) ■ Toilets ■ Disabled access ■ www.rspb.org.uk/reserves-and-events/find-a-reserve/reserves-a-z/reserves-by-name/a/arne/about.aspx

Bardsey Island.

Bardsey Island, Gwynedd

– *24. Tubenose Colony (Manx Shearwater), 30. Rarities*

Bardsey is a stunning island situated just off the tip of the Lleyn Peninsula. Dominated by a large mountain, the island supports a huge colony of Manx Shearwaters which, if staying at the bird observatory, may be visited with the wardens. The shearwater colony is most active between May and August. During spring and autumn the island turns up many migrants, including rarities. Boats depart from Porth Meudwy just south-west of Aberdaron on the Lleyn.

■ For access check Bardsey Island Boat Trips: www.bardseyboattrips.com

■ Information on accommodation: www.bbfo.org.uk/home/4585126036

■ General Island information: www.bardsey.org

Bempton Cliffs.

Bempton Cliffs RSPB, Yorkshire

– *20. Seabird Colony*

250,000 seabirds arrive each summer to breed on the cliffs between here and Flamborough. Highlights include Gannets, Puffins and Kittiwakes. Visit between mid-April and mid-July. The reserve is on the north side of the Flamborough peninsula, 4.5 miles (7km) north of Bridlington and accessed along the signed minor road from the B1229.

■ Free to members (non-members: £3.50 adults, £1.50 children) ■ Car park

■ Toilets ■ Disabled access
■ www.rspb.org.uk/reserves-and-events/find-a-reserve/reserves-a-z/reserves-by-name/b/bemptoncliffs/about.aspx

Bellymack Hill Farm, Dumfries and Galloway – *36. Red Kite*
Bellymack Hill Farm sits 4.7 miles (7.5km) north-west of Castle Douglas, just east of Laurieston, off Kirk Road. The farm is open 12–4pm daily all year with feeding at 2pm. £5 admission (children free) ■ Car park ■ Toilets ■ Disabled access
■ www.bellymackhillfarm.co.uk
■ www.gallowaykitetrail.com/item-38-bellymack-hill-farm-kite-feeding-station

Blackdog, Aberdeenshire
– *19. Displaying Ducks*
Blackdog village is just 1.9 miles (3km) north of Aberdeen and parking can be found by driving through the village off the A90 towards the beach. View seaduck from the dunes or beach. You may have to walk north or south to get closer to flocks. High tide is best as this pushes duck closer inshore, and the greatest numbers are from early autumn until March. Display occurs from January to April.
■ Free ■ Car park ■ No facilities

Blacktoft Sands RSPB, Yorkshire
– *18. Spring Waders, 35. Raptor Roost*
The reserve is at the head of the Humber, just south of the River Ouse, and 5.9 miles (9.5km) east of Goole, off the A161, taking the minor road turning in Swinefleet to the car park just beyond Ousefleet. The reserve boasts many birding highlights so keep your eyes open for Bitterns and Bearded Tits as well waders and raptors. October to March is best for raptor roosts. Arrive one hour before dusk.
■ Free to members (admission charges for non-members) ■ Car park ■ Toilets
■ Disabled access ■ www.rspb.org.uk/reserves-and-events/find-a-reserve/reserves-a-z/reserves-by-name/b/blacktoftsands/about.aspx

Blakeney Point NNR, Norfolk
– *20. Seabird Colony (terns), 30. Rarities*
Managed by National Trust this shingle spit extends for 4 miles (6.4km) parallel to the north Norfolk coast. The terns breed right at the tip of the spit while rarities can be found anywhere along it although the plantation next to the Lifeboat House is one of the best spots. The point can also be accessed by either a long walk from Cley beach or by boat from Blakeney and Morston villages which offers great views of the terns as well as seals. May to August for terns, April to May and mid-August to October for rarities.

■ Free ■ Car parks in Blakeney and Cley
■ Toilets at Lifeboat House on point
■ www.nationaltrust.org.uk/
blakeney-national-nature-reserve

Blean Woods RSPB, Canterbury, Kent – *9. Roding Woodcock, 15. Dawn Chorus, 21. Nightjar*

Blean Woods lies just 1.9 miles (3km) from the centre of Canterbury and is a brilliant example of an ancient woodland crossed by a network of trails. Access off New Road running north-west out of Rough Common. Head out early to enjoy a spectacular dawn chorus. To be in with a chance of Woodcock and Nightjar either arrive just before first light or at dusk. Nightingales may also be heard. If out in darkness hours inform someone of your plans and take a torch.
■ Free ■ Car park ■ Disabled access (limited to certain trails)
■ www.rspb.org.uk/reserves-and-events/find-a-reserve/reserves-a-z/reserves-by-name/b/bleanwoods/

Borth, Ceredigion
– *27. Manx Shearwater aggregations*

Borth lies 6 miles (10km) north of Aberystwyth on the Cardigan Bay coast. The beach extends to Ynylas, which in turn forms the mouth of the Dyfi Estuary. Occasionally in the last couple of weeks of July a huge concentration of Manx Shearwaters can be found feeding on bait fish in the inshore waters along this beach. Check bird information services for updates or head down to the beach to check for yourself.
■ Free ■ Car park ■ Facilities in Borth village

Brampton Woods CWT, Cambridgeshire
– *15. Dawn Chorus (Nightingale)*

Brampton Woods is an isolated ancient woodland (at least 900 years old) 3 miles (5km) south-west of Huntingdon, just south of the A14 and immediately west of the A1. It is accessed from the south side off Brampton Road which leads from Brampton village (exit junction 22 of A14 and enter village on B1514). This cracking reserve managed by the Cambridgeshire Wildlife Trust is a great place to enjoy the dawn chorus (potentially including Nightingales), as well as other woodland wildlife. March to late May is for best for the dawn chorus (April onwards for Nightingale).
■ Free ■ Car park ■ www.wildlifebcn.org/reserves/brampton-wood

Breckland, Norfolk/Suffolk
– *9. Roding Woodcock, 10. Skydancers (Goshawk), 21. Nightjar*

This large district covers the inland areas of Norfolk and Suffolk. Many of the best sites are around Thetford, Norfolk. Here the mosaic of planted coniferous forests and sandy clearings provides superb habitat for Goshawks, while and dusk in summer Woodcock and Nightjars can be seen along the forest rides. Accessible forest tracks and small car parks are dotted throughout the forest. January to March for Goshawk, March to July for Woodcock, and May to August for Nightjar.

■ All facilities in Thetford and surrounding villages. ■ www.norfolkwildlifetrust.org.uk/a-living-landscape/breckland

Brighton Pier, East Sussex
– *34. Starling Murmurations*

Brighton West Pier is home to one of the most famous Starling roosts in the world. The birds can give exceptional views from the promenade as they twist and turn in huge flocks above the town and sea before settling to roost under the pier. Up to 40,000 birds have been counted roosting here. The best murmurations occur from November to March – arrive an hour before dusk for the best show.

■ Free ■ Car park ■ All facilities in Brighton.

Brownsea Island.

Brownsea Island NT, Dorset
– *20. Seabird Colony (terns and gulls)*

Situated in Poole Habour, this island haven teems with life which includes a bustling tern and gull colony (a feature of which are the Mediterranean Gulls). The woodland is also home to many Red Squirrels. The island is accessed by ferries operating from Poole Quay and Sandbanks and includes wheelchair access. April to August for most tern and gull activity.

■ £6.30 adults, £3.50 children (plus ferry fare) ■ Toilets ■ Disabled access ■ Cafe on island ■ www.nationaltrust.org.uk/brownsea-island

Buckenham Marshes RSPB, Norfolk
– *19. Displaying Ducks*

This wetland reserve offers an exceptional duck-watching experience including up to 10,000 Wigeon as well as many other species during winter. It is situated in the Yare Valley of the Norfolk Broads, only 1

mile (1.5km) from Strumpshaw RSPB reserve (which has toilets), and 7.5 miles (12km) east-south-east from Norwich. There is wheelchair access to a small hide. January to March for the best displaying action.
■ Free ■ Car park ■ Disabled access
■ www.rspb.org.uk/reserves-and-events/find-a-reserve/reserves-a-z/reserves-by-name/b/buckenham/index.aspx

Butt of Lewis.

Butt of Lewis, Outer Hebrides
- *30. Rarities, 31. Seawatching*
The Butt lies 20 miles (33km) north of Stornoway at the very northern tip of Lewis, and just 2 miles (3km) north-west of Port of Ness. A car park at the lighthouse offers a possible vantage point for seawatching, or you can walk west for 0.8 miles (1.3km) to the western point which also offers good views. Many rarities have also been found here, especially waders on the short grasslands. The best seawatching follows fast-moving depressions bringing south-westerly followed by north-westerly winds in August to October.
■ Free ■ Car park

Cairngorm.

Cairngorm, Highland
- *11. Grouse (Ptarmigan and Red Grouse)*
While Red Grouse may be found all around the ski centre car park, in particularly cold winters it may also be possible to find Ptarmigan this low down. In general however a walk or ride up Cairngorm is required to see the latter. The funicular railway takes you to the plateau where Ptarmigan can be found, as well as other high-altitude species such as Snow Bunting and Dotterel. Take appropriate precautions and equipment if spending time out on the plateau in wintery conditions. March to May for displaying grouse.
■ Free/Funicular railway: £12 adult, £8 child ■ Car parking ■ Toilets ■ Disabled access ■ www.cairngormmountain.org

Cannock Chase, Staffordshire (Forestry Commission) – *21. Nightjar*

An Area of Outstanding Natural Beauty (AONB) situated just east of the M6 between Stafford and Cannock. Open to the public. Has large areas of suitable heathy and open woodland habitat for Nightjars, but the Sherbrook Valley below the White House Hotel car park is a favoured spot for enjoying them, as well as Woodcock. Another good spot is the Katyn Memorial just east of Camp Road. Check out the Forestry Commission website for guided walks.

■ Free ■ Car park ■ Disabled access
■ www.forestry.gov.uk/birchesvalley

Cemlyn NWWT, Anglesey – *20. Seabird Colony (terns)*

This sheltered lagoon on the north coast of Anglesey is home to 2,500 pairs of Sandwich Terns as well as smaller numbers of Arctic and Common Terns and Black-headed Gulls. Views are superb from the shingle ridge with the colony close by on a protected island. Wardens are on hand to help point things out. Best time to visit is April to August when the colony can appear as complete chaos. From the main A5025 circular road around Anglesey access is signed down the minor road at Tregele. Park in the western car park.

■ Free ■ Car parking
■ www.northwaleswildlifetrust.org.uk/nature-reserves/our-bigger-reserves/cemlyn

Cley.

Cley NWT, Norfolk – *18. Spring Waders*

Probably one of the most famous reserves in the country, Cley has a long history of conservation and producing amazing birding experiences. During May it is one of the best places in Britain to enjoy spring waders (as well as Bittern, Bearded Tit, Spoonbill and many other species). A number of hides offer excellent viewing. The visitor centre is 0.2 miles (0.3km) east of the edge of Cley-next-the-Sea village, immediately on the A149 coast road.

■ Members free (non-members £5) ■ Car park ■ Toilets ■ Limited disabled access
■ www.norfolkwildlifetrust.org.uk/wildlife-in-norfolk/nature-reserves/reserves/cley-marshes

Clocaenog Forest, Denbighshire (Forestry Commission) – *9. Roding Woodcock, 21. Nightjar*

Lying 7 miles (11km) south-west of Ruthin,

this extensive conifer plantation is interspersed with heathy areas inhabited by Nightjars. The wetter areas of woodland also support Woodcock. Churring and roding can be heard and seen from tracks criss-crossing the forest. Best parking at Foel Frech, 3 miles (5km) north of the B5105 – then walk west to listen over the heath. If out at night take a torch and let someone know where you are going.
■ Free ■ Car parking ■ Disabled access (only on public lanes) ■ www.naturalresources.wales/out-and-about/places-to-go/north-east-wales/clocaenog-forest/?lang=en

The Cobbler, Arrochar, Argyll – *11. Grouse (Ptarmigan)*

The Cobbler is one of the more accessible southern Scottish mountains with Ptarmigan. It is not a Munro and therefore is a slightly easier climb. Access is from the car park off the A83 at Succouth, near Arrochar, Loch Long, and involves a 3,020ft (920m) ascent over 7 miles (11km) (return trip). Ptarmigan occur on the tops here and are best found around snowfields.
■ Free ■ Car park ■ Facilities in Arrochar ■ www.walkhighlands.co.uk/lochlomond/the-cobbler.shtml

Colonsay, Argyll – *32. Eagles*

The spectacular island of Colonsay lies in the Hebrides, with Islay to the south and Jura to the east. It is a compact island with only a loop road and restrictions on car access. Bike hire is available. Golden Eagles breed and can be seen well anywhere on the island but try the dunes around Ardskenish in the south-west or Balnahard in the north. Access via Caledonian MacBrayne ferry from Oban or Kennacraig.
■ All facilities on island
■ www.colonsay.org.uk

Conwy RSPB, Conwy – *18. Spring Waders, 34. Starling Murmurations*

This reserve is a brilliant example of what can be achieved out of nothing as it was created in the spoil from the adjacent A55 tunnel. A series of pools and lagoons with patches of reedbed adjacent to the River Conwy draws in hundreds of birds and is the best place in North Wales for spring waders. It is also good for Starling murmurations in winter. It is accessed immediately off the junction 18 roundabout of the A55.
■ Members ■ Free (Non-members: £5 adults, £2.50 children) Car parking ■ Toilets ■ Disabled access ■ Cafe ■ www.rspb.org.uk/reserves-and-events/find-a-reserve/reserves-a-z/reserves-by-name/c/conwy/

Corran Ferry, Great Glen, Highland

– *14. Spring Skuas*

Corran Ferry sits at the head of Loch Linnhe, 8.5 miles (13.5km) south-west of Fort William. Skuas can be viewed from the tiny beach by the ferry car park (sign-posted off the A82 on the A861) as well as from Onich, as they gather at the head of the loch. Other seabirds including divers, Fulmars and terns also pass up the glen from here. Mid- to late May is best for Long-tailed Skuas but other species pass from April.

■ Free ■ Car park ■ Toilets ■ Cafe

Cors Bodeilio NNR, Anglesey

– *22. Nocturnal Marsh Birding*

This stunning reserve is one of the Anglesey Fens. It has an exceptional diversity of plant, invertebrate and bird species and provides the chance to experience nocturnal marsh birding from the boardwalk. Species include Grasshopper, Sedge and Reed Warblers and Water Rail. The site is also good for Glow-worms. The marsh is 2.8 miles (4.5km) east-north-east of Llangefni, and 1.4 miles (2.2km) south-west of Pentraeth along the minor road which turns south off the B5109 through the village housing estate. There is a small car park on the south side of the marsh. Best in April and May.

■ Free ■ Car park (small) ■ Disabled access along short boardwalk.

■ www.first-nature.com/waleswildlife/n-nnr-anglesey-fens.php

Criccieth.

Criccieth Beach, Gwynedd

– *14. Spring Skuas*

Criccieth is a small seaside town on the south-east coast of the Lleyn peninsula. Here skuas migrating north through Cardigan Bay pause before undertaking an overland hop across Snowdonia. The best viewing is from the promenade just west of the castle in May (occasionally also in late April and early June).

■ All facilities in Criccieth

■ www.criccieth.co.uk

Dartmoor.

Dartmoor NP – *9. Drumming Snipe, 11. Grouse (Red Grouse)*

A large expanse of moorland and heath in south Devon. Around 40 pairs of Red Grouse still breed in the heathery areas of the national park. You can access the park on the large number of tracks and footpaths which are accessible from many surrounding roads. The best time to visit is early, around first light, from March to May.

■ All facilities in surrounding towns and villages ■ www.dartmoor.gov.uk

Devil's Bridge, Ceredigion

– *16. Oak Woodland*

This popular tourist destination is 10 miles (16km) east-south-east of Aberystwyth on the A4120. It consists of a series of waterfalls lined by rich Welsh oak woodland. The trails not only give great views of the falls but also the chance to see and hear classic oak woodland species.

■ £3.75 adult, £2.00 child ■ Car parking ■ Toilets ■ Cafe

■ http://devilsbridgefalls.co.uk

Dornoch Beach, Sutherland

– *18. Spring Waders*

The beach lies just to the east of Dornoch town, along beach road. From the car park walk south along the beach. In May Sanderling, Dunlin and Ringed Plover gather in good numbers, offering superb views. In the last few years rarities have also been found here.

■ Free ■ Car park ■ All other facilities in Dornoch

Duncansby Head.

Duncansby Head, Caithness

– *2. Migration, 23. Bonxie, 24. Tubenose Colony (Fulmar)*

The most north-easterly headland on mainland Britain, just 1.2 miles (2km) from John O' Groats. A car park at the lighthouse is right at the centre of the action. The cliffs hold abundant seabirds including Puffins and a high density of Fulmars breeding just to the north of the car park. Bonxies breed on the moors just inland and cruise along the coast here. You can walk south along the cliff-top to give amazing views of the coastal stacks. In September and October the headland can be superb for migrating thrushes, pipits and finches arriving from across the Pentland Firth.

■ Free ■ Car park

Dungeness Bird Observatory, RSPB and NNR, Kent – *14. Spring Skuas, 20. Seabird Colony (terns)*

The best areas for seawatching are from the point where there are two hides. For the spring skua passage use the southern hide. Please visit the bird observatory to arrange access. Peak skua passage is during late April and May. Further birding can be had on the RSPB reserve which hosts a breeding colony of Common Terns between April and August.

■ Free to members/donation ■ Car park ■ Toilets ■ (RSPB) ■ Accommodation at bird observatory

■ www.dungenessbirdobs.org.uk/p/birding-at-dungeness.html

■ www.dungeness-nnr.co.uk

■ www.rspb.org.uk/reserves-and-events/find-a-reserve/reserves-a-z/reserves-by-name/d/dungeness/

Dunnet Head RSPB, Caithness

– *8. Displaying Divers (Red-throated), 20. Seabird Colony, 23. Bonxie, 24. Tubenose Colony (Fulmar)*

Situated 12.5 miles (20km) from Thurso, Dunnet Head is a superbly accessible site from which to view the massive seabird colony, the marauding Bonxies and the entertaining Fulmars. Between May and August the cliffs buzz with life. During these summer months the RSPB staffs a watchpoint and provides viewing assistance; this is a short walk from the car park. Red-throated Divers can be watched from the car on the roadside lochans on the approach road to Dunnet Head car park in May and June. Take the A836 coast road east from Thurso then turn north along the B855 in Dunnet village to the headland.

■ Free ■ Car park

■ www.rspb.org.uk/reserves-and-events/find-a-reserve/reserves-a-z/reserves-by-name/d/dunnethead/

Dunnet Bay, Caithness

– *18. Spring Waders, 19. Displaying Duck, 31. Seawatching*

This large sweeping sandy bay is 9.3 miles (15km) east of Thurso. It's a superb place for northbound waders which often stop off in small tight flocks anywhere along the beach. The best places to see these are the from the western car park at Castlehill, just east of Castletown, and the mid-dunes car park just off the A836. Peak passage is in May. After strong north-westerly winds in autumn many seabirds can get blown into the bay and sometimes offer superb views as they battle back out past Castlehill car park.

▪ Free ▪ Car park

The Exe Estuary at Dawlish Warren.

Exe Estuary, Devon

– *39. Winter Waders*

The estuary supports tens of thousands of waders in winter. Some of the best places to see the huge roosting flocks include The Bight at Dawlish Warren and Bowling Green Marsh RSPB, while the mudflats at Exmouth are good during lower tides. This estuary is superb for wintering Avocets among other species. Why not travel the estuary by train to take in these amazing spectacles?

▪ All facilities available around the estuary, see specific sites for more detail.

▪ www.dawlishwarren.co.uk

▪ www.rspb.org.uk/reserves-and-events/find-a-reserve/reserves-a-z/reserves-by-name/b/bowlinggreenmarsh/

▪ www.avocetline.org.uk/wp-content/uploads/Where-to-watch-birds-leaflet.pdf

Fair Isle, Shetland – *2. Migration, 20. Seabird Colony, 23. Bonxie, 24. Tubenose Colony, 30. Rarities*

Fair Isles is the ultimate birder's island. Situated between Shetland and Orkney it has a phenomenal record of turning up scarce and rare birds. The bird observatory on the island offers very good accommodation and meals as well as all the latest information. While the best time for finding rarities is May to early June and September to October, the island is action-packed from April to October. Access via air or ferry (the Good Shepherd sailing from Grutness, Shetland).

▪ Travel and accommodation costs

▪ One disabled-access room

▪ www.fairislebirdobs.co.uk

▪ www.fairisle.org.uk

Farne Islands.

Farne Islands, Northumberland

– *20. Seabird Colony*

This small archipelago a mile off the coast near the village of Bamburgh is a haven for tens of thousands of seabirds from May to August. It can be reached by boat from Seahouses (additional cost to island fee). Trips normally cruise around the islands before landing on Inner Farne where a boardwalk guides you around the colonies of Puffins, Arctic Terns and gulls. The boat allows close views of breeding auks on the cliffs.

£6.50 adult, £3.00 child, plus boat cost

Toilets (Inner Farne) Check regarding wheelchair access

www.nationaltrust.org.uk/farne-islands

Findhorn Valley, Highland

– *32. Eagles*

Running north-east from Tomatin (on the A9), the Findhorn Valley is an easy stop-off for anyone travelling north or south along this main road. A minor road follows the river upstream and Golden (and occasionally White-tailed) Eagles can be seen over the hills on either side. Watch from the road. Raven, Peregrine and Merlin are also possible here.

Free Car parking (on roadside)

Disabled access

Flamborough Head YWT – *20. Seabird Colony, 24. Tubenose Colony (Fulmar), 30. Rarities, 31. Seawatching*

This amazing promontory, which juts out into the North Sea, harbours thousands of breeding seabirds including Puffins. The head is 5 miles (8km) east of Bridlington. Run by the Yorkshire Wildlife Trust the site is also a hot-spot for rarities in spring and autumn, especially areas such as North Landing and Holmes Gut, while seawatching can prove fruitful in north-easterly winds. The small bird observatory can provide you with extra information.

Donation/Free to members

Car parking Toilets Disabled access Cafe www.ywt.org.uk/reserves/flamborough-cliffs-nature-reserve

http://fbo.org.uk

Frampton Marsh RSPB, Lincolnshire

– *18. Spring Waders, 25. Turtle Dove*

A superb mosaic of wetland habitats that has three hides and a network of paths. The bushes and scrub around the farm fields and visitor centre are a great place to find Turtle Doves in summer from April to September. The turning for Frampton Marsh is signposted off the A16 between Boston and Kirton.

Free (donation from non-members welcome) Car parking Toilets

Disabled access www.rspb.org.uk/reserves-and-events/find-a-reserve/reserves-a-z/reserves-by-name/f/framptonmarsh/

Frenchman's Rocks, Islay, Argyll

– *31. Seawatching*

Situated on the south-west corner of Islay, and accessible via the minor road running out of Portnahaven. From the western limit of the minor road you can park (sensibly on the roadside) and walk 0.3 miles (0.5km) out to the coast, from where you can view out past the three islets and into the Atlantic. In strong westerly and north-westerly winds seabirds are driven along the coast, sometimes between the islets and the main coastline.

■ Free ■ Roadside parking only

Fort George, Moray

– *14. Spring Skuas*

These military battlements sit on a small peninsula that juts out into the Moray Firth 9 miles (15km) north-east of Inverness. Take the A96 along the south side of the Moray then turn north along the B9006 (Military Road) towards the fort. In spring there is the chance of seeing skuas that have passed through the Great Glen emerging here and continuing north-east out to sea. Look south-west from the fort or the shingle car park just before the fort. The skuas may pass over the peninsula. Best time is May.

■ Free (entrance fee to fort) ■ Car parking
■ Toilets and cafe in immediate vicinity

Forvie.

Forvie NNR, Aberdeenshire

– *18. Spring Waders, 20. Seabird Colony (terns)*

Combined with the adjoining Ythan Estuary this is an action-packed section of coast. Well-marked and accessible trails guide you around the reserve and the Dune Trail includes a loop along the estuary. A substantial colony of terns breeds at the river mouth, where there is also a seal colony; this is best viewed from the west side of the Ythan Estuary, from the car park south-east of Newborough. Forvie is 12.5 miles (20km) north of Aberdeen along the A975.

■ Free ■ Car parking ■ Toilets
■ Disabled access
■ www.nnr-scotland.org.uk/forvie/

Foula, Shetland – *20. Seabird Colony, 23. Bonxie, 24. Tubenose Colony (Fulmar), 30. Rarities*

Foula is a wild island situated 17.5 miles (28km) west-south-west of Walls. It's dominated by a large mountain reaching 1,370ft (418m) at the summit of the Sneug. The cliffs of Kame rise 1,234ft (376m) vertically up from the Atlantic, making them the second highest in Britain. You can fly in or catch the ferry, although the latter is highly dependent on good weather conditions. Accommodation is limited to one B&B and a self-catering cottage. You need to take all provisions with you or pre-order from the shop in Walls. During summer the island heaves with birds and the cliffs support over 20,000 pairs of Fulmars – more than any other site in Britain. Add over 1,600 pairs of Bonxies, many Arctic Skuas and of course auks and it makes for a truly spectacular adventure. If you visit in May to June or September to October you may well find some exceptionally rare birds as the island has a remarkable record of turning up vagrants.

■ Travel costs ■ No cars ■ Toilets at airstrip ■ All provisions and accommodation required before visiting unless day-tripping
■ www.foulaheritage.org.uk
■ www.shetland.org/plan/areas/foula

Fowlmere RSPB, Cambridgeshire – *25. Turtle Dove*

This reserve is 8.4 miles (13.5km) south-west of Cambridge and 4 miles (6km) west of the M11. Access is via the north side, off the minor lane between Fowlmere and Melbourn. The rich mosaic of wetland, scrub and woodland habitats makes it a perfect place for Turtle Doves in summer months (mid-April to late August).

■ Donations from non-members
■ Car parking ■ Toilets
■ Disabled access (certain trails)
■ www.rspb.org.uk/reserves-and-events/find-a-reserve/reserves-a-z/reserves-by-name/f/fowlmere/about.aspx

Fowlsheugh RSPB, Aberdeenshire – *20. Seabird Colony*

This brilliant seabird reserve is well worth a visit. It is 3.4 miles (5.5km) south of Stonehaven, with access to the car park signed off the A92 along the minor lane. Walk the 1-mile (1.6km) nature trail to the new viewing shelter to see some of the 130,000 seabirds that come here to breed each year. Keep an eye offshore for Bottle-nosed Dolphins and Minke Whales too.

■ Free (donations welcome) ■ Car parking
■ www.rspb.org.uk/reserves-and-events/find-a-reserve/reserves-a-z/reserves-by-name/f/fowlsheugh/about.aspx

Gibraltar Point NNR and LWT, Lincolnshire – *2. Migration, 18. Spring Waders, 39. Winter Waders*

Gibraltar Point National Nature Reserve is managed by the Lincolnshire Wildlife Trust. It sits on the very northern corner of The

Wash estuary, just 2.5 miles (4km) south of Skegness. The reserve can provide superb views of roosting wintering waders as they gather on the scrapes at high tide. Watch for raptors too. In summer many of the waders look stunning and the reserve is rich in many other species including Little Terns which breed on the shore. In spring and autumn Mill Hill is an excellent spot for watching visible migration. Check out the small bird observatory on site.

■ Parking cost £1 for 2 hours, £3 for the day ■ Car parking ■ Toilets ■ Disabled access ■ Cafe ■ www.lincstrust.org.uk/gibraltar-point ■ http://gibraltarpointbirdobservatory.blogspot.co.uk

Gigrin Farm, Rhyader, Powys

– *36. Red Kite*

As birding spectacles go this is probably one of the best in Britain. In mid-winter as many as 600 kites can wheel around above the farm, which is less than 0.6 miles (1km) from the centre of Rhayader. Kite numbers vary depending on the weather and time of year. The site is open in the afternoons but check the website for the latest feeding times. Specialist photography hides are also available for hire.

■ £6 adults, £4 children ■ Car parking ■ Toilets ■ Disabled access ■ Cafe ■ www.gigrin.co.uk

Goldcliffe Pools, Gwent

– *18. Spring Waders*

These scrapes have proved exceptional for waders in recent years and are well worth checking, especially when combined with the nearby Newport Wetlands RSPB reserve. The village of Goldcliffe lies 3 miles (5km) south-east of the A48 Newport bypass. Arriving from the west you pass the village pub on the left, continue for 0.3 miles (0.5km) over a stone bridge until you reach a small lane on the right. Turn down this and continue for 0.1 miles (0.12km) until you reach a little car park. Pass through the gate to the south and along the bank and you will be able to see the three viewing platforms. Peak passage is during April and May.

■ Free ■ Car park

Goyt Valley.

Goyt Valley, Derbyshire

– *9. Roding Woodcock, 10. Skydancers, (Goshawk), 15. Dawn Chorus*

The Goyt Valley is an extensive site in the Peak District. One of the best areas within it is the woodland around Errwood Reservoir, 3 miles (5km) north-west of Buxton along the A5004. Here the dawn chorus can be superb, especially in May when traffic noise hasn't built up early in the morning. If you arrive early enough or stay until dusk you may also see and hear Woodcock roding here. The area still has a few pairs of Goshawks, although illegal persecution pressures are a huge concern in the area. Keep an eye open above the woodland between February and April for their displays.

■ Free ■ Car parking (Free)
■ Toilets (Derbyshire Bridge car park)
■ www.goytvalley.co.uk

Great Orme – *2. Migration*

A huge limestone headland jutting out into Liverpool Bay and situated immediately north of Llandudno. It holds several sites worth checking and can be accessed either by the coastal one-way lane (Marine Drive), or directly from the south on a minor road which takes you to the summit. Unsurprisingly this very obvious land feature is a great migration point in both spring and autumn. Even watching commoner migrants can be rewarding but scarcities also appear with some regularity. Check the limestone pavement (summit of the north-west tip, reached by a dead-end track) for Dotterel, Richard's Pipit, chats and buntings. The cemetery and scrub to its south-east can be good for warblers, chats and Black Redstart. The gardens of Gogarth on the south-west side are also well worth checking. Peak periods of migration are April to May and August to October

■ Marine Drive £2.50 per car ■ £2 at summit (Free if accessed via Marine Drive)
■ Car parking ■ Toilets (at summit)
■ Cafe at summit.

Great Fen.

Great Fen, Cambridgeshire – *35. Raptor and Crane Roosts*

This ambitious project aims to restore the vast Fenland that once existed between Cambridge and Peterborough. The project area currently envelops several existing reserves to the south of Peterborough. The Wildlife Trust Countryside Centre is a brilliant place to start when exploring this area and offers excellent disability access. Woodwalton Fen NNR provides the best chances of seeing Hen and Marsh Harriers (up to 15 birds) as well as Cranes coming to roost – follow the Marsh Harrier Trail to the northern reedbed. Barn and Short-eared

Owls may be encountered over any part of the Great Fen. Visit between October and March for the highest numbers of roosting raptors.

■ Free ■ Car parking ■ Toilets (Countryside Centre) ■ Disabled access (Countryside Centre and Woodwalton)
■ www.greatfen.org.uk
■ www.greatfen.org.uk/visit/places/countryside%20centre

Greenock, Clyde – *28. Tystie*

Greenock sits on the crux of the Clyde, 22 miles (35km) west of Glasgow. This attractive Scottish seaside town has an esplanade along which you can stroll. Black Guillemots can be seen anywhere along here. At the eastern end they congregate in the small harbour, while peering over the railings at the western end (where the esplanade starts to bend) may bring you eyeball-to-eyeball with an adult keeping watch from its drainhole burrow. Listen out for their high-pitched whistles too. Visit between May and July for the best views.

■ Car parking on the esplanade (may cost)
■ Disabled access ■ Facilities in Greenock

Gretna Green, Dumfries and Galloway – *34. Starling Murmurations*

Lying just within Scotland, Gretna Green on the upper Solway can be home to some astonishing numbers of Starlings. The roost sites vary from year to year and even from week to week, although local residents are likely to know if the roost is situated close to the village. The most frequently used area is just east of the M74 services at Gretna. November to March see the largest numbers.

■ Free ■ Car parking in the village
■ Toilets (in village) ■ Access variable depending on roost location

Graemeshall Loch, Orkney – *19. Displaying Ducks, 29. Swallow Roost*

This small roadside loch is 6 miles (10km) south-south-east of Kirkwall, on Orkney's Mainland. It is best viewed from either the B9052 or Graemeshall Road, which is just to the west. Swallows gather at dusk to roost in the reedbed around the western and northern shores of the loch. The peak period is August.

■ Free ■ No designated parking

Gruinard Bay.

Gruinard Bay, Highland – *32. Eagles*

This large sea loch west of Ullapool has long been a favoured spot for birders to visit in the hope of catching up with eagles, especially White-tailed Eagles. The A832 flanks the southern shores of the loch providing numerous pull-ins and excellent viewing. White-tailed Eagles may be seen anywhere although sometimes multiple birds can be seen gathered on Gruinard Island in the bay. Golden Eagles may be seen over the peaks to the south, and on the approach to the bay from the east. The loch can often hold seaduck, grebes and divers, sometimes including White-billed Diver. Try Loch Ewe to the west for White-tailed Eagles as well.

■ Free ■ Car parking
■ Toilets in Aultbea and Poolewe

Haldon Forest, Devon – *10. Skydancers (Goshawk)*

Located 5.5 miles (9km) south of Exeter, Haldon Forest is a hot-spot for raptor activity. The Forestry Commission has established a raptor viewpoint here which is accessed off the A38 (at the Exeter racecourse junction). Follow the brown signs to Haldon Belvedere. From here follow the signed trails to the viewpoint.

■ Car parking (small charge) ■ Toilets
■ Disabled access ■ Cafe
■ www.dartmoor.gov.uk/__data/assets/pdf_file/0013/41053/au-egdwalk3.pdf
■ www.forestry.gov.uk/forestry/england-devonnoforesthaldonforestparkhaldongate-wayraptortrail

Ham Wall RSPB, Somerset – *9. Drumming Snipe, 22. Nocturnal Marsh Birding, 34. Starling Murmurations*

The newly created wetland has rapidly become one of the best in the UK, supporting myriad species throughout the year from rare breeding herons and egrets in the summer to thousands of Starlings in the winter. Just 2.5 miles (4km) west of Glastonbury, and accessed off Station Road, this flagship reserve offers easy access to the viewing screens, platforms and hides. Why not join one of the organised events to enjoy the starling roost further. The reserve shuts by 10pm in the summer but this allows sufficient time to soak in the dusk and nocturnal sounds.

■ £1.50 per car for 2hours, £3 all day (free to members) ■ Toilets ■ Disabled access
■ www.rspb.org.uk/reserves-and-events/find-a-reserve/reserves-a-z/reserves-by-name/h/hamwall/about.aspx

Hamsterley Forest, Durham – *9. Roding Woodcock, 21. Nightjar*

This extensive conifer plantation 9.5 miles (15km) west of Bishop Auckland is a great place to see roding Woodcock and listen for churring Nightjars in May and June. You can park in the Grove car park, or alternatively listen from the public lane (Windy Bank Road) which runs along the eastern edge of the forest. There is a visitor centre in the east of the forest.

■ Parking charge and toll for forest road ■ Toilets at visitor centre ■ Disabled access ■ Cafe ■ www.forestry.gov.uk/hamsterleyforest

Handa Island WT, Sutherland – *20. Seabird Colony, 23. Bonxie, 24. Tubenose Colony (Fulmar)*

Situated just off the coast of north-west Sutherland, this gem of an island is home to over 100,000 seabirds. It is accessed via pedestrian ferry from Tarbet, 3 miles (5km) north of Scourie. A trail guides you around the island and the reserve wardens will provide you with an introduction on arrival. The island is best visited between May and August.

■ Ferry cost ■ Toilets ■ Visitor shelter ■ http://scottishwildlifetrust.org.uk/reserve/handa-island/

Harris.

Harris, Outer Hebrides – *32. Eagles*

The Isle of Harris sits at the southern end of Lewis (to which it is joined) and is the more dramatic and mountainous part of the island. Try driving the minor road (B887) which runs north-west from the A859 for 2.8 miles (4.5km) to the north of Tarbert. Follow this to Huisinis Beach, keeping your eyes peeled for eagles, especially over the mountains to the north.

■ www.explore-harris.com

Hartshill Hayes, Warwickshire – *2. Migration*

This inland country park is an excellent place to see visible migration. The site is 3 miles (5km) north-west of Nuneaton and accessed from Oldbury Road along the south side of the park. The best time to witness visible migration is from September to November and a good viewing point is the picnic area next to the car park.

■ £2 per car ■ Toilets ■ Disabled access

■ http://countryparks.warwickshire.gov.uk/country-parks/hartshill-hayes-country-park/

Hermaness NNR, Shetland – *20. Seabird Colony, 23. Bonxie, 24. Tubenose Colony (Fulmar)*

Occupying the northernmost tip of Unst, this reserve is home to over 100,000 seabirds including up to 30,000 pairs of Puffins, 16,000 pairs of Gannets and 630 pairs of Bonxies. Park just north of Burrafirth at the head of the road and follow the marked trail over the headland. Walking time is 3–4 hours. Beware of dive-bombing Bonxies, changeable weather and high cliffs.

■ Free ■ Toilets ■ Visitor centre

■ www.nature-shetland.co.uk/snh/hermaness.htm

Hengistbury Head, Dorset – *2. Migration*

The headland is nestled on the Dorset coast near Christchurch. It is one of the best places on the south coast to observe visible migration and on some days thousands of swallows, martins, pipits, Skylarks, pigeons or finches can be seen passing over. Over 100,000 birds have been recorded passing in a single day. Birds typically move into the wind (an easterly direction) and the majority pass in the first hour of daylight. Access to a large car park is along The Broadway from Wick and from here you can walk out over the headland keeping your eyes to the sky for passing migrants.

■ Free ■ Toilets ■ Disabled access

■ Cafe/Visitor centre

■ www.visithengistburyhead.co.uk/Home.aspx

Highnam Woods.

Highnam Woods, Gloucestershire – *15. Dawn Chorus (Nightingale)*

Situated 3.7 miles (6km) west of Gloucester, on the north side of the A40, Highnam Woods is a highly accessible woodland reserve offering superb opportunities for enjoying the dawn chorus with species such as Nightingale and Hawfinch present. The reserve is covered by a network of trails. Why not join the guided walks to see all the woodland has to offer.

■ Free ■ Car parking by prior arrangement only

■ www.rspb.org.uk/reserves-and-events/find-a-reserve/reserves-a-z/reserves-by-name/h/highnamwoods/about.aspx

Hogganfield Loch, Glasgow

– *19. Displaying Ducks*

Just off the M8 in Glasgow, Hogganfield Loch is a particularly accessible city loch that is often teeming with wildfowl. Its urban nature means that many of the wildfowl come to bread, including Pochard, Goosander and Whooper Swan. Between January and March displaying duck can give stunning views. Access the loch from junction 12 of the M8, head north up the A80 for 0.4 miles (0.65km) and turn right into the car park. A tarmac track runs all the way around the loch.

■ Free ■ Car parking ■ Disabled access

Holy Island.

Holy Island, Northumberland

– *30. Rarities*

Holy Island (Lindisfarne) is only accessible at low tide via a causeway (check crossing times before visiting). Once on the island there are numerous areas to check for rarities, not least the extensive sand dunes as you arrive. From the main parking areas on the edge of the village it is possible to loop down Straight Lonnen through the dunes, past the Lough, along the coast and back into the village which covers a number of habitats all worth checking. Best time to visit is April to early June, and mid-August to early November.

■ Car parking (cost) ■ Toilets ■ Cafe

■ www.lindisfarne.org.uk/general/pdf/NNRLindisfarneLeaflet.pdf

Holyhead Harbour, Anglesey

– *28. Tystie*

Holyhead Harbour is the busiest ferry port in Wales yet provides an unlikely southerly outpost for Black Guillemots. They can be seen year-round although in the summer months adults can be found breeding in holes in the harbour walls. The old harbour is generally the most reliable area, especially the fish dock, which is the south-easternmost dock in the harbour.

■ Free ■ Car parking on the dock (park sensibly) ■ Disabled access

Hound Point, Forth – *31. Seawatching*

Undoubtedly one of the best autumn sites for migrating skuas, Hound Point is situated just east of the Forth Bridges at Queensferry and is accessed from the unclassified road immediately under the rail bridge. From this road walk 0.75 miles (1.2km) to the point. Skua passage can occur between early

August and mid-October.

■ Free ■ Parking on unclassified road (do not obscure access)

Hoylake, Cheshire

– 39. Winter Waders

Hoylake town runs along the northern edge of the Wirral Peninsula in Cheshire. At medium and spring tides a huge wader roost is visible right along the shoreline, especially from King's Gap where the North Parade turns inland from the coast. Up to 30,000 Knot as well as Bar-tailed Godwit, Dunlin, Oystercatcher and Ringed Plover gather on the mud and can put on superb aerial displays.

■ Free ■ Parking (may be charged)
■ Disabled access
■ www.deeestuary.co.uk/nwirral.htm

Hyde Park.

Hyde Park and Kensington Gardens, Greater London

– 8. Dancing Grebes, 19. Displaying Ducks, 37. Ring-necked Parakeet

Right in the centre of London, these adjoining royal parks are surprisingly good for birds, not least waterbirds. The Serpentine and Long Water snake through the parks and teems with ducks and grebes, not all of them wild, but at least this allows for very close viewing. Courting Great Crested Grebes may be seen from late winter onwards, as can displaying ducks. It is also possible to hand-feed Ring-necked Parakeets.

■ Free ■ Toilets ■ Disabled access
■ Cafe

Isle of May NNR and Bird Observatory, Fife

– 2. Migration, 20. Seabird Colony, 24. Tubenose Colony (Fulmar)

The Isle of May sits at the mouth of the Firth of Forth, 5.6 miles (9km) south-east of Anstruther on the Fife coast. Access is via boat (fast and slow options) from Anstruther, with another option from North Berwick, Lothian. There is a visitor centre and toilets on arrival and you will be given an introduction to the island by one of the wardens. There are an estimated 45,000 pairs of Puffins, as well as many other seabirds including some particularly obliging Fulmars which can be watched closely at Burnett's Leap. The best months are May to August. There is also a bird observatory on the island but this has no public access.

■ Approx £28 adult and £20 child for boat and island entry ■ Toilets ■ Restricted disabled access – dependent on ferry operators
■ www.nnr-scotland.org.uk/isle-of-may/
■ www.isleofmaybirdobs.org

Isles of Scilly.

Isles of Scilly
– *30. Rarities*

This archipelago off the south-west tip of Cornwall is famed for its balmy climate, tropical-looking seas and ability to turn up rarities. Any of the islands may produce rare birds and the best times are from late March to May and late August to early November. Every habitat can produce birds so it is best to walk slowly and check everything. Access is via air or sea. There is plenty of accommodation on the main islands.
■ www.visitislesofscilly.com

Kew Gardens.

Kew Gardens, Surrey – *19. Displaying Ducks, 37. Ring-necked Parakeet*

The Royal Botanic Gardens at Kew cover a stunning area of cultivated grounds, parkland and woodland which is particularly rich in wildlife. Ring-necked Parakeets are abundant here and can be found in any of the more mature parkland trees. The lakes are good for displaying Mandarin Ducks in February and March. Access off the South Circular (A205) or Kew Road (A307), or more easily by Underground to Kew Gardens station.
■ £9 adults, £3.50 children ■ Car park ■ Toilets ■ Disabled access ■ Cafe
■ www.kew.org/visit-kew-gardens

Kilconquhar, Fife – *29. Swallow Roost*

Kilconquhar is a small village in southern Fife located on the northern shore of a loch of the same name. It is home to a large Swallow roost in August which can be viewed from the parish church grounds or from the minor road immediately east of the village.

- Free
- Limited parking on roadside in village
- Restricted disabled access on road only

Killiecrankie.

Killiecrankie NTS, Perth
– *16. Oak Woodland*

This National Trust for Scotland reserve is situated just west of the A9 between Pitlochry and Blair Atholl. It is accessed by turning off the A9 onto the B8079 to Killiecrankie. The NTS car park is on the left just before the village. The paths guide you through areas of oak, birch, ash and alder woodland with species such as Pied Flycatcher, Redstart and Wood Warbler present. The best time to visit is early morning from late April to early June.

- £2 parking (free to NTS members)
- Toilets
- Cafe
- www.nts.org.uk/Property/Killiecrankie/

Kielder Forest, Northumberland
– *9. Roding Woodcock*

This vast area of forest spans the border of England and Scotland. There are many forestry tracks branching off from minor lanes that cross the forest and you can hear Woodcock roding almost anywhere. Find a safe spot to stand, then listen and watch at dusk for birds displaying.

- All facilities in nearby towns and villages.
- http://visitkielder.com

Kittiwake Tower, Gateshead, Durham
– *20. Seabird Colony (Kittiwake)*

Ten miles (16km) from the coast Kittiwakes have found sanctuary on the quayside of Gateshead. A bespoke Kittiwake Tower was constructed to mitigate the loss of a previous breeding site and now sits on the south bank of the River Tyne at Saltmeadows. Access via Keelman's Way riverside path off South Shore Road. This colony now supports 90 pairs while the extensive colony on the Tyne Bridge – 1 mile (1.5km) upstream – has 250 pairs. Visit between May and July.

■ Free ■ Car parking ■ Disabled access
■ www.gateshead.gov.uk/Leisure%20and%20Culture/countryside/sites/kittiwakes.aspx
■ www.durhamwt.com/kittiwake-cam/

Kelling Heath, Norfolk

– *21. Nightjar*

Immediately south of the north Norfolk coast the Cromer ridge produces some excellent areas of heathland, including Kelling Heath. This can be accessed along the minor road leading due south from the A149 at Weybourne. The minor road splits but both lanes lead up to the heath, however the western fork gives the most direct access along Holgate Hill Lane. Nightjars are almost guaranteed here at dusk in May, June and July. There is a small car park on Holgate Hill Lane where it crosses the heath. Park here and explore the tracks. Take a torch and inform someone of your whereabouts.

■ Free ■ Car parking

Lake Vyrnwy.

Lake Vyrnwy RSPB, Powys

– *10. Skydancers (Hen Harrier and Goshawk), 16. Oak Woodland*

Sunken into the hills of Mid Wales, this large reservoir is surrounded by woodlands and moorland supporting some of the area's most charismatic species, including Red Kite, Goshawk, Hen Harrier, Wood Warbler, Redstart and Pied Flycatcher. Start at the visitor centre on the west side of the dam, and from here you can get up-to-date information on where's best to go. Keep an eye to the sky for displaying Goshawks at the beginning of the year. The woodlands are most active from mid-April to early June. A good option for covering more ground is to cycle around the lake.

■ Free (donations welcome) ■ Toilets
■ Disabled access
■ www.rspb.org.uk/reserves-and-events/find-a-reserve/reserves-a-z/reserves-by-name/l/lakevyrnwy/

Langstone Harbour.

Langstone Harbour RSPB, Hampshire

– *20. Seabird Colony (terns and gulls)*

Easily accessible off the A27 immediately west of Havant and Langstone. Take the A3(M) junction and head east along Harts Farm Way, turning down either of the first two right-hand lanes to car parks on the coastal path. From here you can walk along the coastal path to view the islands which are home to hundreds of breeding terns and gulls between April and August.

■ Free ■ Car parking

■ www.rspb.org.uk/reserves-and-events/find-a-reserve/reserves-a-z/reserves-by-name/l/langstoneharbour/about.aspx

Langdon Beck, Durham

– *11. Grouse (Black Grouse)*

About 15.5 miles (25km) from Barnard Castle, the Upper Teesdale valley is home to a good population of Black Grouse. At Langdon Beck the displaying birds can be viewed from the minor road (B6277) from the safety of the car and without disturbing them. Many males come into the rushy pastures to display and the best time to view is early morning from March until the end of May. The Durham Wildlife Trust organises Black Grouse visits – check their website for more details.

■ Free ■ Limited parking on roadside

Leighton Moss.

Leighton Moss RSPB, Lancashire

– *8. Dancing Grebes, 19. Displaying Ducks, 22. Nocturnal Marsh Birding*

This extensive wetland reserve has a comprehensive network of paths linking the visitor centre to seven hides. The reserve is adjacent to the village of Silverdale, 2.5 miles (4km) west of the M6 and best accessed from junction 35 via Carnforth and Millhead, and then by following Mill Road for 2 miles (3.5km) to Silverdale. The reserve holds many fantastic species including Bittern, Marsh Harrier and Bearded Tit, but it is also a great place to watch grebes and ducks displaying from January through until April. In April and May the reedbeds come alive with the songs of warblers, while Water Rail and Bittern can also be heard during a nocturnal visit (take a torch and inform someone of your route).

■ Hide entry £7 adults, £3.50 children (free to members) ■ Car parking ■ Disabled access ■ Cafe ■ www.rspb.org.uk/reserves-and-events/find-a-reserve/reserves-a-z/reserves-by-name/l/leightonmoss/about.aspx

Lerwick Harbour.

Lerwick Harbour, Shetland

– *28. Tystie*

The capital of Shetland has a bustling port and like many Scottish harbours it is home to Tysties. They may be seen anywhere in the harbour so simply strolling the edge of it gives you the best chance of watching them hunt for Butterfish.

■ Free ■ Car parking on adjacent streets (may be charged) ■ Disabled access Facilities in Lerwick

Llandegla Forest, Denbighshire

– *11. Grouse (Black Grouse)*

Just 5.5 miles (9km) west of Wrexham, Llandegla Forest offers a great opportunity to enjoy Black Grouse lekking from the comfort of a hide. From the visitor centre take the Black Grouse Trail up the hill to the hide on the edge of the moor. The walk is about 2.2 miles (3.5km). Why not join one of the RSPB Black Grouse mornings to learn more about the population here. The forest is signposted off the A525 and access to the visitor centre is down a minor road. You need to be in the hide for dawn to get the most from the experience.

■ £4.50 per car per day ■ Toilets ■ Cafe ■ https://oneplanetadventure.com/walking-routes/

Llanrhidian, Camarthenshire

– *35. Raptor Roost*

This raptor and egret roost is on the north side of the Gower Peninsula close to the small village of Llanrhidian, 9.3 miles (15km) west of Swansea. On arrival in Llanrhidian continue north through the village and out onto Marsh Road (which follows the coast as far as Crofty). Park on the roadside between 0.3–0.6 miles (0.5–1km) from Llanrhidian and scan west across the marshes for raptors coming to roost, including Hen Harrier, Merlin, Peregrine and Short-eared Owl. Best months are October to March.

■ Free ■ Restricted roadside parking

Loch Garten.

Loch Garten RSPB, Highland

– *11. Grouse (Capercaillie)*

Loch Garten is the place to see Capercaillie in the UK. From 1 April to 14 May the reserve opens at 05.30 daily to offer Capercaillie-watching experiences. It is also home to Osprey, Crested Tit and Red Squirrel. The reserve is on the eastern side of Loch Garten, 1.5 miles (2.5km) off the B970 and immediately east of Boat of Garten.

■ £10 adult, £3 concession (free to members) ■ Car parking ■ Toilets ■ Disabled access ■ Visitor centre ■ www.rspb.org.uk/reserves-and-events/find-a-reserve/reserves-a-z/reserves-by-name/l/lochgarten/about.aspx

Loch Gruinart RSPB, Islay, Argyll

– *22. Nocturnal Marsh Birding, 32. Eagles, 35. Raptor Roost*

This large reserve in north-west Islay covers a variety of wetland habitats including estuary, marsh and grazing meadows. In winter it is home to tens of thousands of Barnacle and White-fronted Geese as well as other wildfowl and waders. Heading west out of Bridgend, take the A847 for 2.5 miles (4km) and turn right on the B8017. After 1.5 miles (2.5km) the road flattens out and in winter the marsh on the left can be excellent at dusk for Hen Harrier, Merlin and Barn Owl. Continuing along this road you reach the visitor centre and, up the adjacent minor lane, the bird hides. The tracks to the hides are great in summer for nocturnal marsh birding which can include Corncrake, Water Rail, Grasshopper Warbler and drumming Snipe. The entire area is good for White-tailed Eagles and in winter they will hunt geese and scavenge carrion from the grazing fields and estuary – an impressive sight.

■ Free ■ Car parking ■ Toilets ■ Disabled access ■ www.rspb.org.uk/reserves-and-events/find-a-reserve/reserves-a-z/reserves-by-name/l/lochgruinart/about.aspx

Loch Indaal.

Loch Indaal, Islay, Argyll

– *19. Displaying Ducks*

This huge sea loch splits Islay almost in two. For much of it the A847 runs along its shores and offers many good viewing locations. Some of the best areas are at the northern end of the bay from Blackrock to Bruichladdich. Here flocks of Scaup, Eider, Common Scoter and Red-breasted Merganser can be seen relatively close inshore. January to March is best.

■ Free ■ Car parking on roadside (many pull-ins)

Loch Leven, Perth and Kinross

– *8 Dancing Grebes, 19. Displaying Ducks, 32. Eagles*

Loch Leven is a huge freshwater loch between Edinburgh and Perth. It is accessed off the M90 from junctions 5, 6 or 7. There are many trails around the loch but why not start at Loch Leven RSPB on the south side for up-to-date sightings, hides and a cafe. Other areas to explore include Kirkgate Park at Kinross, and the local nature reserve in the north-west corner. Check out the Heritage Trail for more information. Reintroduced White-tailed Eagles can occasionally be seen hunting over the loch or perched on one of the islands.

■ Prices vary depending on location

■ Car parking throughout ■ Toilets

■ Restricted disabled access ■ www.lochlevenheritagetrail.co.uk/index.html

■ www.rspb.org.uk/reserves-and-events/find-a-reserve/reserves-a-z/reserves-by-name/l/lochleven/about.aspx

Loch of Strathbeg RSPB, Aberdeenshire

– *33. Migrating Geese*

Loch of Strathbeg sits just back from the coast between Fraserburgh and Peterhead. Access is from the A90 at Crimmond from where the reserve is brown-signposted. The best time to visit for migrating geese is September and October when Pink-footed Goose numbers can peak at 80,000 birds. Arrive an hour before dusk to witness them flighting in to the reserve.

■ Free ■ Car parking ■ Toilets

■ www.rspb.org.uk/reserves-and-events/find-a-reserve/reserves-a-z/reserves-by-name/l/lochofstrathbeg/about.aspx

Loch Shin, Sutherland

– *8. Displaying Divers (Black-throated)*

This long – 15 miles (25km) – slim loch nestles in the centre of Sutherland with the town of Lairg at its southern end. A dam separates the main loch from the town and it is on this small area of water that as many as a dozen Black-throated Divers can gather in March and April before dispersing to breeding lochs elsewhere. Arrive at first light for a chance to hear them yodelling across a misty loch and displaying to each other. You can view this area from the pavement of the A836.

■ Free ■ Several small car parks on the edge of the loch ■ Toilets (in Lairg) ■ Disabled access

Lochindorb.

Lochindorb, Moray

– *8. Displaying Divers (Black-throated), 11. Grouse (Red Grouse)*

This moorland loch lies just over 12.5 miles (20km) south of Nairn and is accessed along the A939 by taking the minor road west for 0.3 miles (0.5km), south of where the A940 meets the A939. Continue for 3km until you reach Lochindorb. The divers are best viewed in April and May. Watch only from the road and do not walk along the shoreline as you may cause unnecessary disturbance to this schedule 1 species.

■ Free ■ Car parking on roadside

Lochwinnoch RSPB, Clyde

– *8. Dancing Grebes, 19. Displaying Ducks*

Situated 7.5 miles (12km) south-west of Paisley, off the A737 towards Lochwinnoch village, this wetland reserve is a great place for beginners and more experienced birders alike. A series of lochs and pools provides ample habitat for a variety of species, not least Great Crested Grebes which can be watched displaying on Barr Loch and Aird Meadow.

■ Charge (free to members) ■ Car parking ■ Toilets ■ Disabled access

■ www.rspb.org.uk/reserves-and-events/find-a-reserve/reserves-a-z/reserves-by-name/l/lochwinnoch/about.aspx

The Loons RSPB, Orkney

– *19. Displaying Ducks, 22. Nocturnal Marsh Birding*

The reserve is 11 miles (18km) north of Stromness on Orkney mainland, off the A967 along Loons Road. It is the largest remaining wetland in Orkney and is

excellent all year around. The reserve offers a hide and a viewpoint which are safe to access to enjoy dusk and nocturnal activity.
■ Free ■ Car park (limited) ■ Disabled access from car park to north hide
■ www.rspb.org.uk/reserves-and-events/find-a-reserve/reserves-a-z/reserves-by-name/t/theloons/about.aspx

Lundy.

Lundy Island, Devon
– *20. Seabird Colony*

The island can be accessed by ferry from Bideford and Ilfracombe from mid-March to end of October. It is home to plentiful wildlife, not least seabirds, including Puffins, Guillemots, Razorbills, and more recently breeding Manx Shearwaters. Most of these birds breed on the rugged cliffs on the western side. Once on the island you are free to explore. The 12-mile (19km) ferry journey is good for seabirds (potentially including European Storm-petrel) and Common Dolphins.
■ Return day-trip: £36 adults, £18.50 children ■ Toilets ■ Restricted disabled access ■ Small shop with lunch foods plus pub (serving hot food)
■ www.landmarktrust.org.uk/lundyisland/
■ www.nationaltrust.org.uk/lundy

Machrihanish Seabird Observatory, Argyll – *31. Seawatching*

Situated in south-west Kintyre, this private seabird observatory is well worth a visit. It is a superb example of what can be achieved by a group dedicated of individuals wanting to learn more about seabird migration in an area. A hide has been constructed right on the coast (OS grid reference NR608209) and this can be accessed through Machrihanish village, 5 miles (8km) west of Campbeltown. Follow the minor road which skirts the coast, turning right towards the large warehouses on the coast. Pass by the left-hand side of these buildings and park around the back. The hide is on the small headland here. A westerly or south-westerly gale turning north-westerly is ideal for pushing birds along the coast and right past the hide. These can include Leach's Storm-petrel and Sabine's Gull in August and September. The best movements tend to be at first light.
■ Donations ■ Car parking
■ www.machrihanishbirdobservatory.org.uk/index.htm

Malltraeth Marsh RSPB, Anglesey

– *29. Swallow Roost, 34. Starling Murmurations*

This stunning reserve has been managed to produce a mosaic of wetland habitats. During late summer and winter the areas of reedbed hold roosts of both Swallows and Starlings. Situated just south of the A55, it is best accessed from junction 6 of the A55, then follow the A5 south-east (parallel to the A55) for 1.2 miles (1.9km) across the marsh to a minor turning on the right; take this, and at the next T-junction turn right into the small parking area. From here walk 0.4 miles (0.6km) to the embankment of the Cefni river, then follow the cycle track for 0.8 miles (1.3km) to overlook the reedbed to your south. The embankment gives good height to view over the reeds. Do not leave the cycle track.

■ Free ■ Car parking ■ Disabled access along tracks

■ www.rspb.org.uk/reserves-and-events/find-a-reserve/reserves-a-z/reserves-by-name/m/malltraethmarsh/

Mar Lodge NTS, Aberdeenshire

– *9. Roding Woodcock*

This Highland estate is 3.7 miles (6km) west of Braemar, off the A93. Walk the tracks and lanes at dusk in April and May to be in with a chance of seeing roding Woodcock.

■ Free ■ Car park (£2 non-members)

■ www.nts.org.uk/MarLodgeEstate

Marshside RSPB, Merseyside

– *18. Spring Waders*

This beautiful reserve is the ideal place to experience flocks of spring waders as they stop off on their journey north. Black-tailed Godwits, Avocets and Lapwings mingle together providing excellent views. The reserve lies on the north side of Southport on Marine Drive, only 1.2 miles (2km) from the end of the housing. The main reserve is on the inland side of the seawall. Park in the car park and walk 0.2 miles (0.3km) back to the visitor centre for the latest information and views of the reserve.

■ Free ■ Car parking ■ Toilets

■ Disabled access

■ www.rspb.org.uk/reserves-and-events/find-a-reserve/reserves-a-z/reserves-by-name/m/marshside/about.aspx

Marazion Marsh RSPB, Cornwall

– *22. Nocturnal Marsh Birding, 34. Starling Murmurations*

Sandwiched between Penzance and Marazion village, this wetland reserve can be accessed from the roundabout where the A30 meets the A394. From this roundabout the reserve is only 0.3 miles (0.5km) due south along Newtown lane. Alternatively the reserve can be accessed from the coastal road. The site can be watched from the viewing bays, including one 0.12 miles (0.2km) east of the station car park. At night in April and May listen out for Cetti's, Reed and Sedge Warblers, Bittern and Water Rail. Thousands of Starlings can gather to roost in the reedbed around Christmas and New Year; arrive 1 hour before dusk to watch this spectacle.

- Free
- Car parking (3 private car parks within 100m of reserve, including Marazion railway station car park)
- www.rspb.org.uk/reserves-and-events/find-a-reserve/reserves-a-z/reserves-by-name/m/marazionmarsh/about.aspx

Minsmere.

Minsmere RSPB, Suffolk

– *15. Dawn Chorus, 18. Spring Waders, 25. Turtle Dove*

One of the most famous reserves in Britain. With seven hides and a huge network of trails covering a variety of habitats it never disappoints. The reserve is signposted (brown signs) off the A12 at Yoxford (halfway between Lowestoft and Ipswich). Visit in April and May to see waders looking their most colourful and Turtle Doves purring. Listen out for Nightingales too. Why not join in an event here to get even more out of your visit (see website for details).

- Charges apply for non-members
- Car parking
- Toilets
- Disabled access
- Cafe
- www.rspb.org.uk/reserves-and-events/find-a-reserve/reserves-a-z/reserves-by-name/m/minsmere/about.aspx

Moine Mhore NNR, Argyll

– *9. Drumming Snipe and Roding Woodcock, 17. Cuckoo, 22. Nocturnal Marsh Birding*

Located 5.5 miles (9km) north of Lochgilphead, this extensive lowland raised bog abounds with life during summer. Access along the A816 Lochgilphead to Kilmartin road, then turn south on the B8025 at Slockavulin and continue for 1.2 miles (2km) until the signed car park appears on the left. From the car park take the boardwalk through the birch woodland and out onto the bog. From April to early June the woodland and bog is home to many Cuckoos, while a dusk or dawn visit is likely to give excellent views of displaying Snipe and Woodcock. Grasshopper and Sedge Warblers and Water Rail may also be heard here.

- Free
- Car parking
- Disabled access around boardwalk
- www.nnr-scotland.org.uk/moine-mhor/

Montrose Basin WT, Angus

– *33. Migrating Geese*

This huge estuarine basin is bordered by Montrose town to the east and during autumn is a stop-off point for up to 80,000 Pink-footed Geese. Many also remain for the winter. The main visitor centre is immediately off the A92 on the south side of the basin 1 mile (1.6km) from Montrose. There are hides in other locations too, including on the north-eastern edge of the basin. Get there for dusk or dawn to witness tens of thousands of birds arriving at or leaving the roost site.

- Free
- Car parking
- Toilets
- Disabled access (to some areas)
- http://scottishwildlifetrust.org.uk/reserve/montrose-basin/

Morecambe Bay.

Morecambe Bay, Lancashire/ Cumbria – *39. Winter Waders*

Morecambe Bay is a huge estuary in north-west England which supports thousands of waders (for example, up to 13,000 Curlew, 30,000 Knot and 4,000 Golden Plover). The estuary can be viewed from many points and is at its best for birds between November and March, with most activity an hour before high tide. Key viewing locations include: Hest Bank RSPB, just north of Morecambe; Jenny Brown's Point, Silverdale; Glasson Marsh, 3.7 miles (6km) south-west of Lancaster; and South Ulverston, Cumbria.

Mousa.

Mousa RSPB, Shetland

– *8. Displaying Divers (Red-throated), 23. Bonxie, 24. Tubenose Colony (European Storm-petrel)*

A unique island off the east coast of Shetland, 10.5 miles (17km) south of Lerwick. Accessed via boat from Sandsayre Pier in Sandwick, it is only a short journey across the sound to the island. Once on the island you will find birds breeding everywhere. Bonxies are common and will dive-bomb you. Red-throated Divers breed on the small lochan in the south, close to the Iron-Age broch. You can join an organised dusk trip from the end of May to July to witness the night-time arrival of European Storm-petrels back into the colony. They breed in the broch and surrounding stone walls. When on the island take great care not to disturb breeding birds and at night take a torch to avoid standing on any storm-petrels.

- Ferry: £16 adults, £7 children (£25 adults, £10 children for storm-petrel trip)
- No facilities on the island
- www.mousa.co.uk
- www.rspb.org.uk/reserves-and-events/find-a-reserve/reserves-a-z/reserves-by-name/m/mousa/about.aspx

---

Mull Eagle Watch, Loch Frisa, Mull, Argyll – *32. Eagles*

For a near-enough guaranteed White-tailed Eagle experience head to the watchpoint at Loch Frisa on Mull. The loch is west of the A848 between Salen and Tobermory. The exact location of the watchpoint may change so check the website for details. The period of peak activity is between March and August.

- £8 adults, £3 children
- Car parking
- https://mulleaglewatch.com

Musselburgh Lagoons, Lothian
– *18. Spring Waders, 19. Displaying Ducks*

The lagoons are just 5.5 miles (9km) east of Edinburgh city centre. Access is from the Goosegreen area of Musselburgh (on-street parking), at the mouth of the River Esk. From here walk along the seawall to the east to view the scrapes and sea. April and May are best for waders, January to March for seaduck activity.

- Free
- Car parking

New Fancy View, Forest of Dean, Gloucestershire
– *10. Skydancers (Goshawk)*

This is a great place to see displaying Goshawks from February to April. Here a 360o viewpoint is reached after a short steep climb from the car park. Goshawks can be seen displaying above the forest in any direction. The car park is accessed off the B4226 Cinderford to Coleford road, turning south at Speech House and continuing along the minor road for 1.5 miles (2.5km) until you reach the car park on the left.

- Free
- Car parking

New Forest.

New Forest, Hampshire/Dorset – *9. Roding Woodcock, 10. Skydancers (Goshawk – Acres Down), 21. Nightjar*

The New Forest is a large tract of mixed woodland and heathland covering an area spanning the borders of Hampshire and Dorset. Much of the land is common land and access is easy across most of it. With nearly 600 pairs of Nightjars in the forest it should be easy enough to find your own, however Yew Tree Heath car park, 4.3 miles (7km) south-east of Lyndhurst, is a reliable spot for them. Woodcock can be found roding along woodland edges in similar habitat to Nightjars. The extensive forestry areas are great for Goshawks, which can be seen displaying above the trees from January or February to April. On cold clear mornings try watching for their roller-coastering displays from any open or raised area around Fritham or Acres Down.

■ Free ■ Car parking (may be charged) ■ All facilities in local villages and towns

Newborough Forest.

Newborough Forest, Anglesey – *40. Raven Roost*

This large commercial forest in south-west Anglesey has been planted on an extensive sand dune system. It is a roost-site for Ravens throughout the year, although numbers reach their maximum in January when several hundred birds gather. Park either in the beach car park, which is accessed through Newborough village down a 1.9-mile (3km) road, or from the car parks 1.2 miles (2km) further north in the forestry area. The latter car park requires a 1.5-mile (2.5km) walk south-west down the main forest access track to a rocky bluff on the left of the track. From the beach car park it is worth walking either on the tracks just within the forestry area, or along the beach for 0.9 miles (1.5km). If you get to the site early enough then you may be able to watch Ravens playing in updrafts of the dunes along the second beach (beyond Llanddwyn Island). You can then walk in along the forest tracks in search of roosting birds. Best areas for roosting birds are along the ridges, especially at OS grid reference SH396645.

■ Free ■ Car parking (charged) ■ Toilets (beach car park) ■ Limited disabled access ■ https://naturalresources.wales/out-and-about/places-to-go/north-west-wales/newborough/newborough-forest/?lang=en

Newport Wetlands RSPB, Gwent

– *34. Starling Murmurations*

This brilliant and accessible reserve, situated on the edge of an urban area, is a great place to visit at any time of year, but in autumn and winter the number of birds increases substantially. The reserve can host an impressive Starling roost in the reedbeds so why not check out the website for organised watches or visit late one afternoon to enjoy the spectacle yourself. Access is off the A48 – exit at the Spytty Retail Park roundabout and take the A4810. At the first roundabout take the third exit onto Meadows Road and follow the brown tourist signs.

■ Free ■ Car parking ■ Toilets
■ Disabled access ■ Cafe
■ www.rspb.org.uk/reserves-and-events/find-a-reserve/reserves-a-z/reserves-by-name/n/newportwetlands/about.aspx

Norfolk Broads.

Norfolk Broads, Norfolk

– *9. Drumming Snipe, 22. Nocturnal Marsh Birding*

An extensive area of reedbeds, shallow artificial lakes and other wetland habitats east of Norwich. There is access in many areas, such as Wroxham, Brundall, Acle and Potter Heigham, and there is also a plethora of reserves including Hickling, Strumpshaw and Buckenham Marshes. As well as the reserves there are also public footpaths along many of the bunds which allow safe access to great areas for nocturnal marsh birding, including the hide at Rush Hill Scrape which is best accessed by parking at the church at Potter Heigham and walking north along the footpath to Hickling Broad bund – turn right for Rush Hill (OS grid reference TG423209). Strumpshaw RSPB reserve is also god for nocturnal birding.

■ Free ■ Car parking (some may be charged) ■ Other facilities limited

North Ronaldsay, Orkney

– *31. Seawatching*

North Ronaldsay is the northernmost island on Orkney and possibly the best seawatching location in Scotland. Birds can cut close to the island as they head out of the North Sea and into the Atlantic. The best spots for viewing are between the old and new lighthouses, however the former is very close to sea-level which can make viewing tricky in big seas. The best conditions tend to be strong south-easterly winds, but westerlies and north-westerlies are also good. Peak time for seawatching is between August and early October. If you stay on the island there is accommodation at the bird observatory.

■ Free ■ Limited access and facilities at the seawatching locations

■ www.the-soc.org.uk/birding-north-ronaldsay/

■ www.nrbo.co.uk

Noss Head, Caithness – *2. Migration, 33. Migrating Geese*

Extending 2.8 miles (4.5km) north-east of Wick, this large headland is a hot-spot for bird migration. Access is through Wick town to Papigoe and on to Staxigoe where a sharp left turn leads you all the way to the car park near the tip of the headland. From here you can walk to the lighthouse. Migrating geese can be seen following the coast south in September and October and it is also worth checking for other migrants in the bushes by the car park and around Noss Farm (do not enter the farm itself).

■ Free ■ Car park ■ Disabled access along road

Noup Head RSPB, Westray, Orkney – *14. Spring Skuas (including Long-tailed Skua)*

Westray lies in the north-west of the archipelago and is accessible by air or sea. In recent years Noup Head, the most north-westerly promontory, has been identified as a good spot from which to observe Long-tailed Skua migration in May. From Pierowall village turn left at the school, following signs for Noup Cliffs. Turn left at the junction past Noltland Castle, continue up the hill and through Noup Farm and follow the gravel track to the parking area at the lighthouse.

■ Free ■ Car parking

■ www.rspb.org.uk/reserves-and-events/find-a-reserve/reserves-a-z/reserves-by-name/n/noupcliffs/about.aspx

Oban Harbour.

Oban Harbour, Argyll – *28. Tystie*

A hub of ferry activity on the west coast of Argyll where Black Guillemots can be seen at any time of year from the promenade. Access via the A85 and A816. There is ample parking along the sea front. Ideal for combining with a trip to the Hebrides.

■ Free ■ Car parking (charged) ■ Toilets ■ Disabled access ■ Cafes

Otmoor RSPB, Oxfordshire
– *25. Turtle Dove, 34. Starling Murmurations*
Just 5 miles (8km) north-east of Oxford and close to the M40, this low-profile reserve is a superb site to enjoy Starling murmurations in winter and the soft purrs of Turtle Doves in summer. Access from the A34 (junction 9 on M40), then take the B4027 south through Islip and continue along the B4027 towards Wheatley. After 4 miles (6.5km) turn left to Horton-cum-Studley, then turn left to Beckley. After one mile the road drops down a short steep hill. Turn right before the Abingdon Arms. Turn sharp left into Otmoor Lane, follow the road to the end – about 1 mile (1.5km) – and turn left into the reserve. The car park is on your right.
■ Free ■ Car parking ■ Disabled access (not possible in winter when tracks are muddy) ■ www.rspb.org.uk/reserves-and-events/find-a-reserve/reserves-a-z/reserves-by-name/o/otmoor/about.aspx

Oxford University Museum of Natural History.

Oxford University Museum of Natural History, Oxford – *26. Swift*
Oxford was the first 'Swift City' in Britain, so what better than to visit the founding place for Swift research, the university museum. Here 60 pairs breed in the ventilation flues in the roof, where they have been studied since 1947. You can watch the Swifts (and also view them on the webcam) at any time of day between May and August but their dusk return to the breeding holes is worth staying for. The museum is a 15-minute walk from Oxford city centre, just off Parks Road.
■ Free ■ Car parking on nearby streets
■ www.oum.ox.ac.uk/visiting/swifts/
■ www.rspb.org.uk/our-work/rspb-news/news/425109-oxford-to-become-englands-first-swift-city

Parkgate Marsh, Cheshire
– *35. Raptor Roost*
This site can be good at any time, especially between October and March, but on a few occasions each year spring tides push across the marsh and force the birds closer to the observers. The Parade runs along the seawall at Parkgate, which is west of the A540 (the main western arterial road on the Wirral). On particularly high tides the marsh is lost and there is no raptor roost here, but at other times raptors can be pushed a little closer than normal. Hen and Marsh Harriers, Merlin, Peregrine and Short-eared Owls are all regular.

Free · Car parking · Disabled access on The Parade
www.rspb.org.uk/reserves-and-events/events-dates-and-inspiration/collections/deeestuary.aspx

Peedie Sea, Kirkwall, Orkney – *19. Displaying Ducks*
The Peedie Sea is situated on the western edge of Kirkwall town, in a town park with easily accessible concrete tracks around the western edge. It is the best place in Britain to see what are effectively urban Long-tailed Ducks, as well as other diving and dabbling ducks, including sawbills. Visit between January and April for the best shows of duck display
Free · Car Park · Disabled access

Pendeen.

Pendeen, Cornwall – *31. Seawatching*
This is one of the best places in Britain for close views of seabirds. The headland is accessed through Pendeen village, 7.5 miles (12km) north-west of Penzance. At the crossroads at Higher Boscaswell turn north and continue for 1.5 miles (2.5km) until you reach Pendeen Lighthouse. Park here and walk out to the point (OS grid reference SW378359) just behind the lighthouse. Best conditions are generally following the movement of an anticyclone across southern Britain when south-westerly winds turn north-westerly and push birds close in past the headland. A trio of rocks offshore helps with directions too. July to September tend to be the best months.
Free · Car parking

Penmon Point.

Penmon Point, Anglesey – *28. Tystie*
Home to the southernmost Tysties in Britain, this attractive headland at the eastern tip of Anglesey is 4.3 miles (7km) from Beaumaris. Turn from the B5109 between Beaumaris and Llangoed and follow for just over 1.2 miles (2km) to the T-junction. Turn right and continue along this road to Penmon Priory. You can either park at the priory and walk, anord drive to the point and park. The fast-flowing water

between the point and Puffin Island is good for Tysties as well all other auks. Walk the northern coast to increase your chances of seeing them.

■ Charged (rates vary depending on parking location) ■ Car parking ■ Limited disabled access ■ Toilets in cafe at point

Point of Ayr RSPB, Flintshire

– *39. Winter Waders*

Reached off the A548 down Station Road to the end of Talacre, this coastal reserve is a hot-spot for wader activity. Parking is at the end of the road and a 0.6-mile (1km) track takes you along the seawall to a viewing platform overlooking the saltmarsh. Arrive about an hour before high tide to witness the waders gathering. November to March is best for big numbers.

■ Free ■ Car parking ■ Disabled access ■ www.rspb.org.uk/reserves-and-events/find-a-reserve/reserves-a-z/reserves-by-name/d/dee-pointofayr/about.aspx

Portland Bill, Dorset

– *2. Migration, 14. Spring Skuas (including Pomarine), 30. Rarities*

The Isle of Portland juts out into the English Channel from the Dorset coast. It is a birding hot-spot, brilliant at any time of year but particularly good in the peak migration periods. Turn south off the A35 and follow the A354 from Dorchester all the way to Portland. The bird observatory should act as a focal point for you, a good way of gleaning up-to-date information and seeing some ringing in action. From here explore the many fields and lanes for migrating birds and search for rarities among them. The best migration periods are March to May and August to November. In late April and May a good passage of Pomarine Skuas can be seen from the Bill if conditions are right (south to south-easterly wind).

■ Free ■ Car parking ■ All facilities on Isle of Portland ■ Accommodation available at Bird Observatory

■ http://portlandbirdobs.blogspot.co.uk/p/home.html

Porthgwarra, Cornwall

– *31. Seawatching*

Lying south-east of Land's End, Porthgwarra is less dependent on weather than nearby Pendeen. The best conditions are south-westerlies between July and October although southerlies can also be good. Ideally the low pressure system should hit the 'toe' of Cornwall directly and the best days involve squally showers and more prolonged bands of rain. This is a particularly good site for large shearwaters. Turn south off the B3315 at the crossroads 0.2 miles (0.3km) west of Tretheway village and continue for 1.5 miles (2.5km) to the beach car park at Porthgwarra. From here

walk south-south-west over the heath to the rocks above Hella Point (OS grid reference SW370215) to the best seawatching spot.
■ Free ■ Car parking (charged) ■ Toilets

Portree Harbour.

Portree, Skye – *32. Eagles*

This lively Scottish town is a brilliant base from which to explore the island and also to see eagles. Just stepping out of any accommodation or building gives you a good chance of seeing the White-tailed and Golden Eagles that breed close by. You can scan from the pier towards the cliffs at the harbour mouth; drive to the Aros Centre 0.6 miles (1km) outside town, where you can learn a bit about local heritage as well as scan anywhere around you; or you can take either the Brigadoon or Stardust boat trips out to get close-up views of at least White-tailed Eagles (see Organisations and contacts for more details of these boat trips). Eagles can be seen year-round but December to February often prove to be the best times.
■ All facilities in Portree
■ www.isleofskye.com/portree

Red Kites Wales Feeding Station, Llandeusant, Brecon Beacons
– *36. Red Kite*

This site is in the heart of the Brecon Beacons National Park. Feeding occurs daily at 3pm BST and 2pm GMT so it's worth being on site early to see the start of it. To access the site from Brecon travel west along the A40 and turn left at Trecastle. Follow the road for 8.7 miles (14km) into Llanddeusant, then turn right for Myddfai (by the camping park). The feeding station is 0.12 miles (0.2km) on the right. Feeding occurs all year.
■ £4 adults, £2 children ■ Car parking
■ Toilets ■ www.redkiteswales.co.uk/red_kites_information.html

Richmond Park, Surrey
– *37. Ring-necked Parakeet*

This extensive park in south-west London is home to hundreds of Ring-necked Parakeets which can be found breeding in the large trees scattered throughout. The A3 cuts straight through the park or it can be accessed via Richmond Underground station or mainline train stations. Visit at any time.
■ Free ■ Car parking ■ Disabled access
■ Toilets ■ Cafe
■ www.royalparks.org.uk/parks/richmond-park

Rum.

Rutland Water.

Rum, Highland – *24. Tubenose Colony (Manx Shearwater)*

Located just south of Skye in the Sea of the Hebrides, this dramatic island is an apt setting for watching thousands of shearwaters returning to their burrows. The island is reached from Mallaig by ferry (Caledonian MacBrayne, but charters are available). Once on the island you will need to make your way to the higher parts where shearwaters breed. The best access is from Kinloch in the east. It is a good idea to join an organised tour – visit the reserve office in Kinloch for more information. The best time to experience the shearwaters is after dark between June and August.

■ Free (but transport to and accommodation on the island is required)

■ www.isleofrum.com/pulsepro/data/img/uploads/files/Manx%20Shearwaters%20SNH%20Leaflet.pdf

Rutland Water, Rutland – *8. Dancing Grebes, 18. Spring Waders*

As well as being famous for hosting the British Birdwatching Fair every August, Rutland Water has a superb reserve with 31 hides and is a great place to see migrating waders in spring. The reserve is best accessed south of Oakham along the A6003, taking the turning east to Egleton along Hambleton Road for 0.6 miles (1km) to the car park. There is also a visitor centre at Lyndon Road, accessed along the south side of the reservoir. Turn off the A6003 at Manton and continue for 1.4 miles (2.2km) to the crossroads (just beyond the garden centre). Turn north to the visitor centre at the end of the lane (signposted). Peak wader passage is late April and May. Dancing grebes are best between February and May.

■ £5.70 adults, £3.30 children (discount for Leicestershire and Rutland Wildlife Trust members) ■ Car parking ■ Toilets

■ Disabled access

■ www.rutlandwater.org.uk/visitor-info/

Saltcoats Harbour, Ayrshire
- *14. Spring Skuas (including Long-tailed Skua)*
Sitting on the coast at the north end of the Firth of Clyde, Saltcoats town is perhaps an unlikely location for skua passage but in May (generally the last two weeks) it can sometimes prove spectacular for Long-tailed Skuas. Watch from the green on the small headland (north side of the harbour) where the Premier Leisure Cinema is situated (off The Braes/Winton Circus). Get there at first light to maximise your chances. Other skuas are also seen here with the commoner species being noted from April.
■ Free ■ Car parking ■ Disabled access

Selsey Bill, Sussex
- *14. Spring Skuas (including Pomarine Skua) 33. Migrating Geese*
With large wintering populations of Brent Geese along the south coast a good passage of birds can be seen during September and October as birds arrive from the Arctic. Selsey Bill is a prime viewing spot, located 7.5 miles (12km) south of Chichester off the A27. Take the A286 south, turning after 0.3 miles (0.5km) onto Selsey Road and continuing all the way to the end of Selsey town. You can watch from the beach at the old cricket ground, or from any beach just along the eastern side of the peninsula (south end of Selsey Promenade). Geese often move by low over water to the west. The site is also noted for its passage of Pomarine Skuas in late May.
■ Free ■ Car parking
■ Limited disabled access

Severn Beach, Gloucestershire
- *31. Seawatching*
Right at the top of the Severn, immediately before the Severn Bridge on the English side, Severn Beach can be a superb seawatching site during strong south-westerly winds, especially between August and November but occasionally also through the winter too. Watch from the Severn Way, where Station Road meets the coast.
■ Free ■ Car parking ■ Toilets in train station (150m) ■ Disabled access

Sheringham.

Sheringham, Norfolk
- *31. Seawatching, 33. Migrating Geese*
Located 3.7 miles (6km) west of Cromer, the seaside town of Sheringham is a great place for seawatching and autumn goose migration. It can be reached either along

the A149 coast road or off the A148. Once in the town park on the Esplanade and drop down the ramp to the coastal huts, promenade and buildings. There are several open shelters with seats that are perfect for seawatching. The best time is August to October, while peak movement for goose flocks is September and October. Watch out for other wildfowl and waders on the move as well.

■ Free ■ Car parking (charged) ■ Toilets ■ Disabled access

Slapton Ley.

Slapton Ley NNR, Devon – *29. Swallow Roost*

A long lagoon trapped by a shingle bank 22 miles (35km) south-east of Plymouth. Access to this remote area is via any number of back roads but the easiest is off the A34 through Avonwick, Diptford, Moreleigh and down to Slapton. This historic Swallow roost has been well studied by the field centre researchers present on site for many years. The best experiences occur in August and September. Park at Memorial car park (at the top end of the lagoon on the beach) and cross Slapton Bridge, then walk 0.5 miles (0.8km) along the edge of the lagoon to overlook the reedbed. The Swallows can be seen gathering over the lagoon from about one hour before dusk before dropping into the reeds.

■ Free ■ Car parking ■ Toilets (Torcross and Memorial car parks)

■ www.slnnr.org.uk

Slimbridge WWT, Gloucestershire – *19. Displaying Ducks, 35. Crane Roost*

This mecca for birders has a year-round plethora of experiences to enjoy. Wildfowl make up the bulk of the interest and it's a great place to see ducks displaying in late winter and early spring. Additionally it has become the easiest place in Britain to see Common Cranes, and up to 16 have been seen at any one time. They can be seen throughout the year. Slimbridge is best accessed off junction 13 of the M5, turning north onto the A419 and then taking the first exit at the roundabout. After 3.4 miles (5.5km) take the third exit at the roundabout in Slimbridge (signposted to WWT Slimbridge). Follow this lane for 2.2 miles (3.5km) to the car park.

■ £11.03 adult, £6.08 child ■ Car parking ■ Toilets ■ Disabled access ■ Cafe

■ www.wwt.org.uk/wetland-centres/slimbridge/

Skomer Island WTSSW, Pembrokeshire – *20. Seabird Colony*

Access to Skomer is by day-trip from Martin's Haven, 2 miles (3.2km) west of Marloes village, which is 12 miles (19km) south-west of Haverfordwest. Boats run from Tuesday to Sunday between 1 April and 30 September, and on Monday there is a round-island cruise that also visits Grassholm (which is also superb for seabirds and has a huge gannetry). It is worth booking boat trips in advance and you also need to purchase landing fees from Lockley Lodge in Martin's Haven before departing. Peak time to visit is May to the end of July. There is also overnight accommodation.

■ Landing fee (free to members): £10 adults, £5 children; Boat fare: £11 adults, £7 children ■ Car parking £5 all day ■ Toilets ■ www.welshwildlife.org/skomer-skokholm/skomer/

Skokholm, Pembrokeshire – *24. Tubenose Colony (Manx Shearwater and European Storm-petrel)*

Much like nearby Skomer this island is a haven for seabirds and not least Manx Shearwaters. To properly experience these birds you need an overnight stay as day-trips and incidental landings are not permitted. You can book three-, four-, or seven-night stays here. The wardens will also take you out to show you storm-petrels and shearwaters in their burrows (this is the only place in Britain where you can see storm-petrels in their burrows). Boat arrangements will be confirmed when booking.

■ Starting from £110 for 3 nights, £27.50 for boat ■ Parking on mainland at West Hook Farm (£8 per night) ■ All facilities on island ■ www.welshwildlife.org/skomer-skokholm/skokholm/

Snettisham.

Snettisham RSPB, Norfolk – *18. Spring Waders, 39. Winter Waders*

Snettisham is perhaps the best place for watching wader activity in the whole of Britain. At the highest tides waders are pushed off the mudflats of the Wash and between 30–90 minutes before high tide the birds start flooding over the seawall and onto the scrapes. Watch the initial exodus from the estuary from Wader Watchpoint while the viewing screen at the southern end of Pit 4 is the best once birds are on the scrapes. During May there aren't as many birds present but those that are look stunning. The biggest numbers (up to

50,000) occur between August and January. To access Snettisham turn west off the A149 at Snettisham (signed) down Beach Road and park on your left in the reserve car park.
■ Free ■ Car parking ■ Restricted disabled access
■ www.rspb.org.uk/reserves-and-events/find-a-reserve/reserves-a-z/reserves-by-name/s/snettisham/about.aspx

Solway Viaduct, Cumbria
– *14. Spring Skuas*

Situated on the south side of the Solway Firth estuary, 0.6 miles (1km) west of Bowness-on-Solway village, this site has an excellent record of producing spring skua passage and especially Pomarine Skuas. The viaduct, labelled as Herdhill Scar on OS maps, is best accessed from the minor road leading west from Bowness, along the footpath. Skua passage normally commences around 20 April and lasts until end of May. The best conditions occur following the movement of deep depressions off south-west England which push birds into the Irish Sea. A continued south-westerly helps push birds up the Solway, and these then circle to gain height and pass north-east over land. This site is exposed.
■ Free ■ Car parking restricted on roadside

Sound of Gigha, Argyll – *8. Displaying Divers, 19 Displaying Ducks*

This sheltered stretch of water between Gigha and Kintyre is a superb area for ducks and divers. During winter groups of Long-tailed Duck, Common and Velvet Scoters and Eider, as well as sawbills, gather off the coast while Great Northern Diver numbers can exceed 400 during winter months.
In spring it can be brilliant for summer-plumaged divers (all three species). Check Rhunahaorine Point, accessed through Point Sands Holiday Park.
■ Free ■ Car parking at Point Sands but check access on arrival

South Stack.

South Stack RSPB, Anglesey
– *24. Tubenose Colony (Fulmar), 20. Seabird Colony*

Situated just 2.5 miles (4km) west of Holyhead, this fantastic reserve hosts thousands of seabirds between April and August. There are several car parks, an excellent visitor centre (Ellen's Tower) and great cafe, plus steps leading down the side of the cliffs to the lighthouse. Here you can get brilliant views of auks and Fulmars at eye-level. It is also one of the best places in Britain to see Chough. Follow the brown tourist signs out of Holyhead along South Stack Road to the reserve. Fulmars can be seen from February. Take care along unprotected cliff edges.

Free ■ Car parking ■ Toilets
■ Restricted disabled access ■ Cafe
■ www.rspb.org.uk/reserves-and-events/find-a-reserve/reserves-a-z/reserves-by-name/s/southstackcliffs/about.aspx

Spurn Peninsula, Yorkshire

– *2. Migration, 26. Swifts, 30. Rarities*

Rapidly becoming a destination of choice for many birders, this phenomenal peninsula is incredibly rich in both birds and birders, with a super observatory which also hosts the Spurn Migration Festival. Spurn is 22 miles (35km) east of Hull – take the A1033 to Patrington, then the B1445 to Easington and south to Kilnsea. The new observatory offers comfortable accommodation while day-trippers can still enjoy ringing demonstrations. Swifts pass through the in June and July, while peak months for other migrants are generally late March to the end of May and mid-August to the end of October. Rarities tend to turn up in these peak migration periods.

■ Free (day-trip), from £20pppn in observatory ■ Car park ■ Toilets
■ www.spurnbirdobservatory.co.uk

St John's Pool, Caithness

– *18. Spring Waders, 19. Displaying Ducks, 20. Seabird Colony (terns)*

Located on the edge of St John's Loch, Brough, approximately 11 miles (18km) east of Thurso, this private reserve is a superb site to watch gulls, terns, waders and ducks in close proximity from the comfort of the hides. There are also two water-level photography hides available for use (pre-booking only). February to May for displaying duck, April to August for terns and May for waders.

■ Free ■ car park ■ Disabled access
■ www.stjohnspool-birds.co.uk

St Kilda, Outer Hebrides

– *20. Seabird Colony, 23. Bonxie, 24. Tubenose Colony (Leach's Storm-petrel and Fulmar), 30. Rarities*

Situated 50 miles (80km) west of the island of Harris and only accessible by boat. Day-trips can be arranged from Harris and Uig, Skye. Camping is permitted by prior arrangement. St Kilda is home to vast numbers of seabirds and offers an array of experiences. It is however an expensive place to visit.

■ Expensive boat access only ■ Toilets
■ www.kilda.org.uk

Stodmarsh.

Stodmarsh NNR, Kent

– *29. Swallow Roost, 35. Raptor Roost*

This superb large wetland is situated close to Stodmarsh village, 4.3 miles (7km) north-east of Canterbury, and is networked by public footpaths. The site holds many important breeding and roosting species and well as being good for invertebrates and plants. Access off the A28 at Grove Ferry and also from Stodmarsh village, which is located further along Grove Road.

- Free
- Car park (fee at Grove Ferry)
- Disabled access
- http://publications.naturalengland.org.uk/publication/35044?category=59026

Strid Wood, Yorkshire

– *15. Dawn Chorus, 16. Oak Woodland*

A beautiful example of oak woodland in the Yorkshire Dales between Bolton Abbey, Barden Bridge and Wharfedale. It's a great place to experience oak woodland avifauna and dawn choruses. Take the B6160 off the A59 at Bolton Bridge and continue north for 1.5 miles (2.5km), parking at Cavendish Pavilion.

- Free
- Car park (may be charged)
- Toilets
- Cafe
- www.natureinthedales.org.uk/get-involved/places-to-see-wildlife/strid-wood-and-the-strid

Strid Wood.

Strumble Head.

Strumble Head, Pembrokeshire

– *31. Seawatching*

This lighthouse peninsula sits 4.7 miles (7.5km) north-west of Fishguard. The road ends in with two car parks and seawatching is best from the old modified WW2 searchlight station where shelter can be found. Best conditions are a westerly to north-westerly wind following a south-westerly blow.

Free Car parking

Stubb Mill NWT, Norfolk

– *35. Raptor and Crane Roosts*

Park at the Norfolk Wildlife Trust centre at Hickling Broad and walk 1km to the raised viewing platform. Do not drive to the platform. Wellies are recommended as it can get muddy. Try and arrive one hour before sunset to enjoy the best of the spectacle. The car park is accessed down Stubb Road, out of Hickling, 2.5 miles (4km) north of the A149. Best time to visit is November to March.

Free car parking Toilets

www.norfolkwildlifetrust.org.uk/wildlife-in-norfolk/nature-reserves/reserves/hickling-broad

Sumburgh Head.

Sumburgh RSPB, Shetland

– *20. Seabird Colony, 24. Tubenose Colony (Fulmar)*

Three viewing platforms allow superb views of the seabird colony and there is often an information warden on hand to provide assistance, identification tips and direct you to the best spots. The reserve is located at the very southern tip of Shetland Mainland.

Free Car park (limited)

www.rspb.org.uk/reserves-and-events/find-a-reserve/reserves-a-z/reserves-by-name/s/sumburghhead/

Sutcliffe Park, Greater London

– *37. Ring-necked Parakeet*

Sutcliffe Park is sandwiched between the A2 and A20, just east of the A2213 which connects the two. Ring-necked Parakeets roost in the tall trees in the centre and around the edge of the park. The roost is best visited between November and March.

Arrive at least an hour before dusk to witness the birds arriving.

■ Free ■ Car parking ■ Disabled access

Taynish NNR, Argyll
– *15. Dawn Chorus, 16. Oak Woodland*

Situated 13 miles (21km) from Lochgilphead and 1 mile (1.6km) south of Tayvallich. It is an exceptional example of northern rain-forest, and during spring and summer is crammed full of woodland flowers as well as birds. Best visit at dawn from mid-April to the end of May.

■ Free ■ Car park

■ www.nnr-scotland.org.uk/taynish/visiting/trails/

Thurso Bay, Caithness
– *19. Displaying Ducks*

This relatively small bay is bounded by Scrabster to the west and Thurso and Thurso River mouth to the south and east. It is an excellent place to enjoy great views of Long-tailed Duck, Eider, Common and Velvet Scoter and Red-breasted Merganser. Birds can be seen all around the bay but some of the best viewing is from the mouth of the Thurso River. Keep an eye open for rarer winter gulls, divers and waders too. January to April is the peak period for ducks.

■ Car park ■ Toilets (Thurso River mouth)

■ Disabled access

Tiree.

Tiree, Inner Hebrides – *30. Rarities*

A low-lying predominantly agricultural island in the Inner Hebrides. Its position means that it can be directly on the route of incoming birds from North America and also those migrants that filter down the west coast of Scotland. There are several reserves, some with access, as well as many good beaches and gardens to watch.

■ Access via air or sea ■ All facilities

■ www.isleoftiree.com

Titchwell RSPB, Norfolk
– *18. Spring Waders*

With state-of-the-art hides, easy access and a deluge of birds, Titchwell is one of the RSPB's centrepiece reserves. It is situated on the north Norfolk coast, 6 miles (10km) east of Hunstanton and just off the A149. Worth a visit at any time of year but waders in late April and May can be in stunning plumage.

■ Free ■ Car parking (non-member charge) ■ Disabled access ■ Toilets

■ Cafe
■ www.rspb.org.uk/reserves-and-events/find-a-reserve/reserves-a-z/reserves-by-name/t/titchwellmarsh/

Trotternish.

Trotternish, Skye, Inner Hebrides – *32. Eagles, 33. Migrating Geese*
This huge peninsula, lying due north of Portree, is dominated by a spectacular ridge and massive cliffs that are home to both species of eagles. In autumn geese following the Minch and the sea lochs south can filter along both the east and west sides of Trotternish. Any prominent vantage point, or for instance the head of Loch Snizort, provides a good opportunity to watch geese as they arrive in September and October. Eagles can be seen anywhere along the peninsula. Facilities are available in Uig and Portree. For latest sightings and more information on the area see: www.skye-birds.com

Troup Head, Aberdeenshire – *20. Seabird Colonies, 31. Seawatching*
The head offers some great opportunities to enjoy seabirds including breeding Gannets and Puffins. Viewing is from the coastal path. The reserve is positioned directly between Banff and Fraserburgh on the north coast of Aberdeenshire, 11 miles (18km) east of Banff. A signposted minor road off the B9031 takes you to the car park.
■ Free ■ Car park
■ www.rspb.org.uk/reserves-and-events/find-a-reserve/reserves-a-z/reserves-by-name/t/trouphead/about.aspx

Tollie Red Kites RSPB, Dingwall, Sutherland – *36. Red Kite*
This feeding station is located 4 miles (6.5km) south-west of Dingwall and provides a great opportunity to see Red Kites up close. The site is signposted off the A835. Check the website for feeding times. The peak period of kite activity is normally between November and March.
■ Free ■ Car park ■ Toilets
■ www.rspb.org.uk/reserves-and-events/find-a-reserve/reserves-a-z/reserves-by-name/t/tollieredkites/about.aspx

Wells Wood, Norfolk – *30. Rarities*
A long swathe of planted pine forest on the sand dune system of Holkham, lying 2 miles (3.2km) north-west of Wells-next-the-Sea on

the north Norfolk coast. In the autumn this forest can hold many scare and rare birds. Favoured areas include The Dell towards the eastern end of the forest and the western edge of the forest where it meets the dunes.

■ Car park (Lady Anne's Drive and Wells beach) Toilets

■ www.holkham.co.uk/nature-reserve-beach/nature-reserve/introduction

West Loch Tarbert, Kintyre, Argyll

– *8. Displaying Divers*

This sea loch sits at the north end of the Kintyre Peninsula to the west of Tarbert. It is particularly sheltered and offers great feeding for many birds throughout the year. During summer non-breeding divers and off-duty breeding birds frequent the sea loch and can give superb views in any part of the loch, especially at high tide. Parking is possible at Ronachan on the south side, and along minor northern road. The best period for summer-plumaged divers is April to July.

■ Free ■ Car park ■ Toilets (Kennacraig ferry terminal)

Westhay/Shapwick.

Westhay Moor SWT/NNR, Somerset

– *9. Drumming Snipe, 35. Raptor and Crane Roosts*

Close to Ham Wall, this reserve is best accessed off the M5 at J23. Follow the A39 east for 6.2 miles (10km) to Wood Lane and into Shapwick, then turn north along Station Road, leading into Shapwick Road, into Westhay, continue north on the B3151 for 0.5 miles (0.8km) and turn onto West Moor Drove. The car park is 1.1 miles (1.8km) along the road at junction with Dagg's Lane Drove. Watch over the reedbeds and willow carr for up to an hour before dusk between October and March for Hen and Marsh Harriers, Merlin, Peregrine and Barn Owl; Common Cranes also roost here.

■ Free ■ Car parking

■ www.somersetwildlife.org/westhay_moor.html

Wheldrake Ings YWT, Yorkshire

– *22. Nocturnal Marsh Birding*

This superb wetland site is 8 miles (13km) south-east of York in the Derwent Valley. Access from the A64 along the A19 to Crockey Hill. Turn east and continue for 3.7 miles (6km) into Wheldrake, carrying on through and along Church Lane for 0.5 miles (0.8km) to the car park on the left. Peak months are April to June when a walk along the trails could produce a variety of nocturnal songsters from rails and crakes to warblers and waders. If out at night take a torch and inform someone of your plans.

■ Free ■ Car parking ■ Disabled access

■ www.ywt.org.uk/reserves/wheldrake-ings-nature-reserve

Whitehall Wood, Hertfordshire

– *36. Red Kite*

Between Luton and Stevenage the small woodland of Whitehall (OS grid reference TL171238) is an excellent roost site for Red Kites with up to 100 birds present on some evenings. The site is 1.9 miles (3km) west of the B651, close to Preston village. Arrive an hour before dusk to witness the birds arriving to roost.

■ Free ■ Roadside parking

Wildboarclough, Macclesfield, Cheshire – *15. Dawn Chorus*

This small hamlet is 5 miles (8km) south-east of Macclesfield at the edge of the Peak District, accessed off the A54. All the minor roads around this village are surrounded by woodland and it makes a superb place to listen to the dawn chorus. Get there before sunrise between late March and end of May to make the most of it.

■ Free ■ Roadside parking

Wood of Cree.

Wood of Cree RSPB, Dumfries and Galloway – *16. Oak Woodland*

A classic oak woodland dominated by bluebells in May. It is accessed through Newton Stewart, crossing the river on the B7079 and taking the first left north along the Cree for 3.7 miles (6km) until you reach the car park. Visit between late April and early June to experience the best of this site.

■ Free ■ Car parking

■ www.rspb.org.uk/reserves-and-events/find-a-reserve/reserves-a-z/reserves-by-name/w/woodofcree/about.aspx

Wormwood Scrubs, Greater London

- 37. Ring-necked Parakeet

This park is situated in west London just north of the A40 (Westway). Take Wood Lane north to Scrubs Lane. Alternatively you can catch the underground to East Acton then walk 0.2 miles (0.3km) north-east along Erconwald Street to reach the park. Peak activity is between November and March. Get there an hour before dusk to see the parakeets arriving.

■ Free ■ Limited car parking
■ Disabled access

Wykenham Forest, Yorkshire

- 10. Skydancers (Goshawk)

A raptor watchpoint situated 10km west of Scarborough in the North Riding Forest Park. The car park is at OS grid reference SE943882 and there is an easy access path leading up to the watchpoint where Goshawks and Honey Buzzards may be seen. It is best accessed via the minor road off the A170 at Wykenham village. Try late January to April for Goshawk display and May to June for Honey Buzzards.

■ Free ■ Car parking ■ Disabled access
■ www.forestry.gov.uk/forestry/englandnorthyorkshirenoforestwykehamforestraptor-viewpoint

Ythan Estuary, Aberdeenshire

- 18. Spring Waders

See Forvie NNR for details.

SCOTLAND

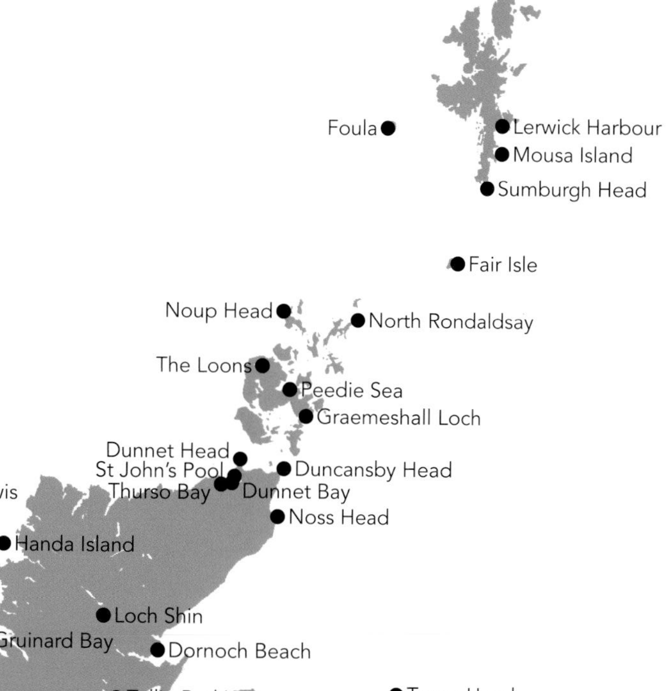

Hermaness
Foula
Lerwick Harbour
Mousa Island
Sumburgh Head
Fair Isle
Noup Head
North Rondaldsay
The Loons
Peedie Sea
Graemeshall Loch
Dunnet Head
St John's Pool
Duncansby Head
Thurso Bay
Dunnet Bay
Butt of Lewis
Noss Head
Handa Island
St Kilda
Loch Shin
Gruinard Bay
Dornoch Beach
Harris
Aird an Runair
Trotternish
Tollie Red Kites
Troup Head
Fort George
Loch of Strathbeg
Portree Harbour
Applecross Mountain
Lochindorb
Findhorn Valley
Forvie/Ythan
Blackdog

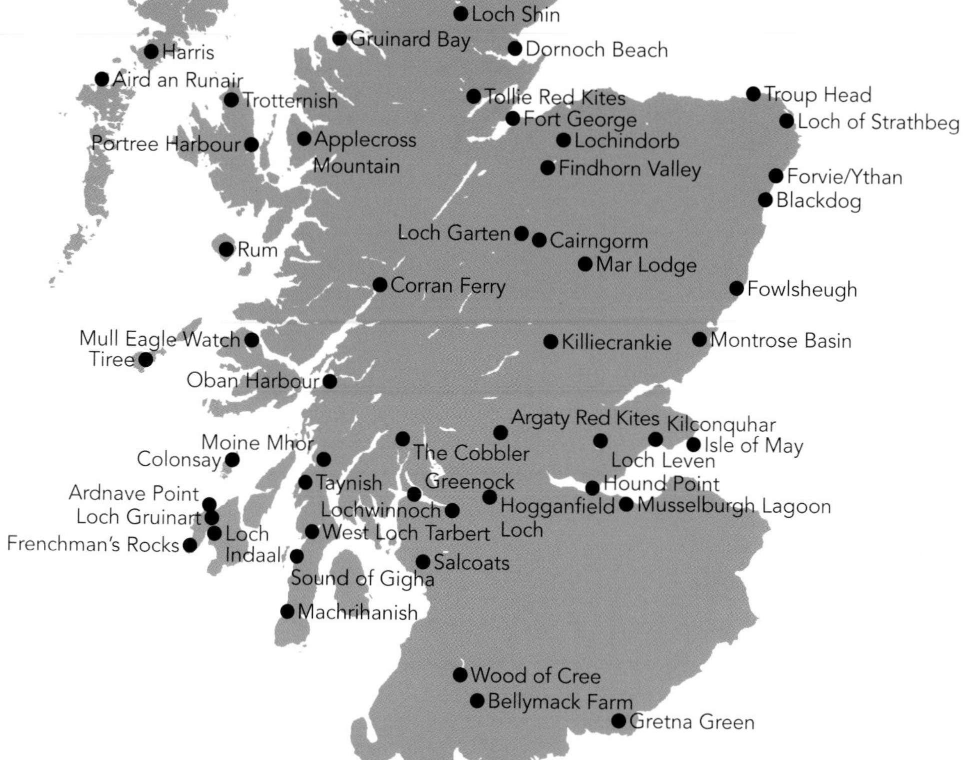

Loch Garten
Cairngorm
Rum
Mar Lodge
Corran Ferry
Fowlsheugh
Mull Eagle Watch
Tiree
Killiecrankie
Montrose Basin
Oban Harbour
Argaty Red Kites
Kilconquhar
Moine Mhor
Isle of May
Colonsay
The Cobbler
Loch Leven
Ardnave Point
Taynish
Greenock
Hound Point
Loch Gruinart
Lochwinnoch
Hogganfield Loch
Musselburgh Lagoon
Frenchman's Rocks
Loch Indaal
West Loch Tarbert
Salcoats
Sound of Gigha
Machrihanish
Wood of Cree
Bellymack Farm
Gretna Green

ENGLAND
Holy Island
Farne Islands
Keilder Forest
Kittiwake Tower
Solway Viaduct
Hamsterley Forest
Langdon Beck
Bempton Cliffs
Wykenham Forest
Leighton Moss
Flamborough Head
Morecambe
Strid Wood
Wheldrake Ings
Blacktoft Sands
Spurn Peninsula
Marshside
Titchwell
Wells Wood
Hoylake
Goyt Valley
Blakeney Poi
Cley
Parkgate Marsh
Wildboarclough
Gibraltar Point
Kelling He
Frampton Marsh
Snettisham
Sheringha
Cannock Chase
Hickling Broad
Rutland Water
Buckenham Marshes
Harthhill Hayes
Great Fen
Norfolk Borads
Breckland
Brampton Woods
Minsmere
Whitehall Woods
Highnam Woods
Otmoor
New Fancy View
Slimbridge
Oxford Natural History Museum
Wormwood Scrubs
Hyde Park
Severn Beach
Kew Gardens
Sutcliffe Park
Stodmarsh
Richmond Park
Blean Woods
Lundy Island
Westhay
Ham Wall
Dungeness
Langstone Harbour
New Forest
Brighton Pier
Selsey Bill
Exe Estuary
Hengistbury Head
Dartmoor
Haldon Forest
Brownsea
Slapton Ley
Arne
Portland Bill
Pendeen
Marazion
Porthgwarra
Isles of Scilly

WALES

Cemlyn
Holyhead Harbour
South Stack
Penmon Point
Cors Bodeilio
Malltraeth Marsh
Newborough Forest
Great Orme
Conwy
Aber Valley
Point of Ayr
Clocaenog Forest
Llandegla Forest
Criccieth Beach
Bardsey Island
Lake Vyrnwy
Borth
Aberystwyth
Devil's Bridge
Gigrin Farm
Strumble Head
Red Kites Wales Feeding Station
Skomer Island
Skokholm Island
Llanrhidian
Newport Wetlands
Goldcliffe Pools

Organisations and Businesses

There are a host of organisations, businesses and media that can enhance your birding experiences; here are some of the most useful ones in Britain. Here are some of the most useful ones in the UK, *or those mentioned within this book.*

Bird Observatories Council – the body overseeing the management and running of the UK's bird observatories. www.birdobscouncil.org.uk

Birdfair – the biggest and best celebration of everything to do with birds, held annually at Rutland Water in August. www.birdfair.org.uk

Birdguides – online bird news and articles. www.birdguides.com

Brigadoon Boat Trips – based in Portree, Skye, and offer an opportunity to see White-tailed Eagles from the sea. www.portree-boat-trips.co.uk

British Trust for Ornithology (BTO) – science-focused ornithological charity coordinating all the main atlasing and population trend studies. www.bto.org

British Birds Rarities Committee (BBRC) – the body that assesses rare bird occurrence in the UK. www.bbrc.org.uk

Great Crane Project – responsible for implementing the Common Crane reintroduction. www.thegreatcraneproject.org.uk

Hawk and Owl Trust – charity dedicated to conserving owls and birds of prey in the UK. www.hawkandowl.org

Nest Record Scheme – a subset of the BTO responsible for collating bird nesting data. www.bto.org/volunteer-surveys/nrs/about

Patchwork Challenge – an informal annual competition for people who watch a local patch. http://patchworkchallenge.blogspot.co.uk

Rare Bird Alert – a news and sightings service. www.rarebirdalert.co.uk

Royal Society for the Protection of Birds (RSPB) – the largest conservation organisation in the UK with over 1 million members. www.rspb.org.uk

Sealife Surveys – based in Tobermory, Mull, and offer an opportunity to see White-tailed Eagles from the sea as well as seabirds. www.sealifesurveys.co.uk

Sound Approach – a company established to aid our understanding of bird sound. https://soundapproach.co.uk

Spurn Migration Festival – annual festival celebrating migration at Spurn, Yorkshire, including ringing demonstrations, talks and lots of great birding. http://spurnmigfest.com

Stardust Boat Trips – a good opportunity to see White-tailed Eagles from the sea off Portree, Skye. www.skyeboat-trips.co.uk

Where's The Path – free online OS and comparative satellite mapping of Britain. https://wtp2.appspot.com/wheresthepath.htm

The Wildlife Trusts – large wildlife conservation organisation with county or regional conservation initiatives as well as country-wide programmes. www.wildlifetrusts.org

Woodcock Network – A brilliant site detailing the work being undertaken on Woodcock in the UK. www.ringwoodcock.net

Xeno-canto – the largest source of online bird sounds. http://xeno-canto.org

IMAGE CREDITS

Dan Brown: pages 102–103. John Davis: pages 130, 131. Dreamstime.com (individual photographer names in brackets): front cover (Portland Bill) (Andrew Martin); front cover (swifts), pages 6, 9, 13, 48–49, 55 above, 55 below, 75, 83, 89, 90, 99, 105, 114, 125, 128, 134, 162, 171, 180, 181, 183 (Mikelane45); 10 (Peter Smith); 11 (Andrew Astbury); 17, 137, 156, 157 (Thomas Langlands); 23 (Shabra); 25 (Ian Keirle); 27 (Onefivenine); 46 above (Urospoteko); 46 below (Alexander Erdbeer); 50, 60 below (Lee Amery); 51, 57 (Wkruck); 66, 160–161 (Juha Saastamoinen); 67 (Gisli Baldursson); 69 (Andrew Sproule); 71 (Vasiliy Vishnevskiy); 76 (Boris Belchev); 82 (Tomasztc); 86 (Marilyn Barbone); 87 (Stillwords); 98 (Christopher Lindner); 104 (Gail Johnson); 106 (Isselee); 109 (Vlasenko); 113 (Joan Egert); 116 (Dalia Kvedaraite); 121 (Martin Pateman-lewis); 127 (Farmdogfan); 139 (Péter Gudella); 149 (Tapichar); 153 (Neil Burton); 155 (Rinus Baak); 158–159 (Paul Farnfield); 174 (Brackishnewzealand); 176 (feathercollector); 179 (19838623doug); 184 (Louise Roach); 186 (Keithpritchard). Stephen Duffield /Western Isles Wildlife: page 79. Conor John: pages 20–21. Simon Papps: page 33. Magnus Robb, page 47. Shutterstock.com (individual photographer names in brackets): pages 2–3 (Jesus Giraldo Gutierrez); 5 (jennyt); 14 (Mark Bridger); 15 (Neil Burton); 18–19 (Hartmut Albert); 26 (michaket); 28 (Kazakov Maksim); 29 (Alexander Erdbeer); 31 (Roby1960); 35 above, 144, 145, 146 (Tony Mills); 35 below, 96 (Martin Pelanek); 37, 42 (Nick Vorobey); 39 (Pan Demin); 40 (Tom Reichner); 41 (tahirsphotography); 43 (Wilfred Marissen); 45 (bearacreative); 52 (Patryk Kosmider); 53, 91, 95, 112 (Dzmitry Yakubovich); 60 above (Dennis Jacobsen); 63 (aaltair); 64 (Wang LiQiang); 70 (eWilding); 73, 135, 170, 211, 224, 237, 240 left (Erni); 77, 185 (Marcin Perkowski), 80, 110 (BMJ); 81 (Wolfgang Kruck); 84 (Fidel); 92 , 202 right (Francesco de Marco); 94 (Menno Schaefer); 97 (Ivan Kuzmin); 100 (grusgrus444); 111 (KOO); 117, 119 (Miroslav Hlavko); 122 below (Steve Pleydell); 126 (Gallinago_media); 13–141 (Keith Pritchard); 138 (shaftinaction); 140–141 (Vishnevskiy Vasily); 142–143 (Michael Schroeder); 150 (Mateusz Sciborski); 152 (Denisa Mikesova); 154 (Vladimir Kogan Michael); 163 (Richard Evans); 164 (Pefkos); 166 (Pajda83); 167 (Mark Medcalf); 169 above (Szczepan Klejbuk), 169 below (Rainer Fuhrmann); 172–173 (Ian Sherriffs); 177 (Kazakov Maksim); 188–189 (Peteris Dancs); 191, 243 (Joe Dunckley); 192 left (JuliusKielaitis); 192 right (Geoffrey Keith Booth); 195 (allou); 196 left (Richard Bradford); 196 right (Duncan Andison); 197 (Ernie Janes); 199 (travellight); 200 left (Ian Woolcock); 200 right (Jaroslav Sekeres); 202 left (Andrew Roland); 204 (Alex C Stuart); 206 (David Hughes); 207, 235 (J and S Photography); 208 (David Falconer); 210 (Anneka); 212 (Michael Conrad); 213 (MJSquared Photography); 214 left (James LePage); 214 right (Cristian Gusa); 215 (Claire Fraser Photography); 216 (Y Bwthyn Photos); 217 left (Simev); 217 right, 225 left (Kevin Eaves); 218 (Bildagentur Zoonar GmbH); 219 (Jan Holm); 220 (Pearl Bucknall); 221 (Philip Bird LRPS CPAGB); 222 (Diana Mower); 225 right (TTphoto); 226, 228 (Helen Hotson); 227 (matt_train); 229 (David Falconer); 230 (Pajor Pawel); 231 left (Simon Burt); 231 right (phildaint); 233 (Sue Stokes); 234 left (Martin Gillespie); 234 right (Julie Cutler); 236 (Gordon Bell); 238 (Gail Johnson); 240 right above (P.D.T.N.C.); 240 right below (salpics32); 241 (Paul Riddell); 242 (Alistair MacLean); 244 (Ian Redding); 245 (ASC Photography). Brydon Thomason/Shetland Nature: pages 122 above, 123.

INDEX

Note: Birding sites are listed alphabetically in the gazetteer, and cross-referenced with the experience accounts (and on the maps). Locations mentioned or pictured incidentally in the text are listed in the Index. **Bold** page number = image.

First published in 2017 by Reed New Holland Publishers

London • Sydney • Auckland

The Chandlery, 50 Westminster Bridge Road, London SE1 7QY, UK
1/66 Gibbes Street, Chatswood, NSW 2067, Australia
5/39 Woodside Avenue, Northcote, Auckland 0627, New Zealand

www.newhollandpublishers.com

A record of this book is held at the British Library and the National Library of Australia.

ISBN 978 1 92151 775 4

Group Managing Director: Fiona Schultz
Publisher and Project Editor: Simon Papps
Cover Design: Andrew Davies
Designer: Catherine Meachen
Production Director: James Mills-Hicks
Printer: Toppan Leefung Printing Ltd

10 9 8 7 6 5 4 3 2 1